Acker

ADVANCED PRAISE FOR *ACKER*

A spiraling jackdaw of cross genre writing, Douglas A. Martin's *Acker* combines close reading, biography, and personal journal into a work as obstreperous and polyvocal as his subject, Kathy Acker. Like Acker, Martin breaks frame and convention to invoke the subject herself, "Acker," an author who slipped in and out of character to careen polymorphous and vagrant across the seams of multiple narratives. Martin writes an intimate portrait of *the subject in question* by drawing on himself as *a* writer reading *the* writer, in a hide and seek in which identities switch and serially peel, in an homage that elides boundaries of form, narrative distance, and readerly absorption. —Erica Hunt

In *Acker*, Douglas A. Martin does what he's always done— he explores and explodes the personal (in this case Acker, in this case himself) to pinpoint not one easy universal truth but a multitude of very difficult truths. Providing a harmonious antidote to the personality of Acker herself through a sort of asynchronous and timeless historical and critical account and with oceanic brilliance in thinking and writing that is unparalleled, Martin fills in the spaces of her life that we yearned for in other attempts to tell her tale with a true depth of character—both his own and hers, and ours. And in this contemporary moment, he gives us the gift of this book—as Acker might have wanted to do herself—to fill us again with the demons of hope and inspiration and with the hard-earned lessons of a life absolutely lived. —Dorothea Lasky

This is a book worthy of its subject: singular, unpredictable, a mongrel that occupies that rare, evocative space between genres. Expressing truths that transcend the stolid facts of conventional biography and literary analysis, Douglas A. Martin reveals how the act of writing is also, always, an act of self-authorship, of identity destruction and creation—and how Acker took this process to an extreme that still stuns, confounds, and inspires. —Astra Taylor

Acker

DOUGLAS A. MARTIN

NIGHTBOAT BOOKS
NEW YORK

ISBN: 978-1-937658-71-7

Design and typesetting by HR Hegnauer

Cover: *Queen of Lights*, from *The Outsider Tarot*,
   by Bobby Abate, 2017

Cataloging-in-publication date is available
from the Library of Congress

Distributed by the University Press of New England
One Court Street
Lebanon, NH 03766
www.upne.com

Nightboat Books
New York
www.nightboat.org

for Toby & Amy

In writing, the point is not to manifest or exalt the act of writing, nor is it to pin a subject within language; it is, rather, a question of creating a space into which the writing subject constantly disappears.

Michel Foucault

We want to explode the frigid, inhibited, mortified body that capitalism wants so desperately to make out of our living body.

Guy Hocquegnghem

PART ONE

The Poet and the Novelist

1.

A fact I had to frame: I believe she died November 30, 1997, in Tijuana, Mexico. A brief, lucid essay featured in *The Guardian*, where while living in England she also contributed book reviews, "The Gift of Disease," outlined the grounds for a courageous, if life-altering decision she made to turn her back on Western medicine and to pursue, as she had for the entirety of her writing career, alternatives. The choice would be taken up for further debate in those pages. Jeanette Winterson came to a defense, stating, "Kathy wanted to be ill in the way she wanted to be well: on her own terms." Biographer Jason McBride gives her reported last words and adjusts the date of death to December 1. Was she someone to follow in the footsteps of? Was she someone to let have a say for us, to accompany us through days, to take living cues from, someone to see an emerging self reflected in, who we might then try to emulate. Resigned finally to a hospital, lungs filling up and needing to be drained, she died not long after someone coming in to do her nails had made her quite happy. This I could know from a letter in her papers, left by an executor's brother or sent later, to let him know. *Eurydice in the Underworld* (1997): *...Is she nothing / Or is she your mirror?*

2.

One "I'm born" in *The Childlike Life of the Black Tarantula by the Black Tarantula,* by Kathy Acker, comes closest perhaps or indeed is the truth: April 18, in the year of 1947. But note a birth there too, "in the late autumn or winter of 1827," as another narrating **I** confesses. Before long, another *I* joins that one, for a next section of part one of the work: *I'm born poor St. Helen's,* *the Island of Wight. 1790.* And again in a third section of the first part, another birth is given: *I'm born in Holly Springs, Mississippi, in 1837.* In a footnote to the opening of a collection of critical essays on Acker (2004, *Devouring Institutions*, Hardin) meant only to be an introduction to her work, the editor cites birth years appearing variously as 1943, 1944, 1945. Exactly where this is does not get clarified, and those places might very well be the fictions. Acker would fill her novelistic enterprise with such autobiographical tease. In her version of *Great Expectations*, the narrator, as her Tarot, "a psychic map of the present, therefore: the future," is being read, refers to April 18 as her significator. Birth certificate, driver's license, and passport give 1947 for the author's birth year, according to Acker's literary executor Matias Viegener. Her Library of Congress information lists 1948. Her major U.S. publisher, Grove Press, takes the later date in a biographical note on the back of a first edition, trade paperback, of two posthumous titles together in one volume: *Rip-off Red, Girl Detective* and *The Burning Bombing of America: The Destruction of the U.S.* In one of Acker's last novels, *My Mother: Demonology*, one of her narrative strategies has become to now *redo* her "childhood"—which within the work means to include a set of memories, and dreams, and pieces written or rewritten when younger—and then the starting point for a life narration changes yet again: *I was born on October 6, 1945.*

3.

"I lie on the grass a stake through my heart I am every woman," she writes in *The Burning Bombing of America: The Destruction of the U.S.*, speculated to originate from 1972, formulating among other ideas—the betrayal of friends, revolution, total chaos—a communistic (socialist) embrace. AMERICA: *what is communism about? the desire of the heart for more than one love.* AMERICA: *how does one (we) recover? I change identity.* She would become a bit of a one-woman identity factory, to forever spin out some new configuration.

4.

In *The Childlike Life of the Black Tarantula*, we move from ideas of murderesses. These are individuals, even if historic, now in Acker's life in part because she has begun to investigate or to invest in them. We move when the book moves to San Francisco to ideas of lesbians, though these are not equivalencies. They are movements through time and place, such a day and age, exploring instead what one might have been. When she does fictionally confine herself to more just among women, her developed characteristic dynamics play in ways more abjectly humorous and cartoonish. This would be all of *Pussy, King of the Pirates* (1996), a landmark and last novel she published in her life, after its opening preface ending: *I stood on the edge of a new world.*

5.

In a telling interview performed with publisher and theorist, friend and once lover, Sylvère Lotringer, Kathy Acker agrees: "I act through the novels." Their chat opens her 1991 collection, *Hannibal Lecter, My Father*. I find him to provocatively comment after having recently seen some early video footage of his addressee, "that is how I like you," in a letter stored away in the archive of her papers at Duke University, remarking on that rare combination of "tough and tender" that was hers. The intersection of these two qualities acquire symbolic and surreal, spectacular materiality on the cover of the first U.S. edition of her 1993 novel, *My Mother: Demonology*. From an aerial view, a bit of sidewalk like two legs meeting up where they split, we see coming into design around a patch of grass bush furred, groomed into almost the perfect triangle, only with softer points and tips. "Two white roses rise out of the small squares of wet soil placed in the concrete," she writes in the late "Eurydice" piece, an image she then develops and reinforces: *I once said 'a rose is my cunt.'* She gives the qualities I begin here to trace also to the rebel James Dean, love a cause, to think-slash-say about Janis Joplin, in a rehearsal of those two stars who would become major characters in one of the latter movements of the Acker work *The Adult Life of Toulouse Lautrec by Henri Toulouse Lautrec*: "She really was a softy kid even though she pretended to be so tough," an early manuscript in the Serpent's Tail/High Risk Archive at Fales Library, NYU. The family romance that comes to develop in Acker is through projection onto such stars, filmic, mythic, and literary, cultured underground. Then there also exists a seeing-through this a bit. Dean as figure of comparison recurs in the aftermath of one of the cruising scenes Acker has her sailors do, before moving more from them to a camp of pirates. James Dean is in *My Mother: Demonology*, as well as in "Requiem" (1997), where the logic goes: "*Billy looks exactly like the person she dreams is her ideal brother of all time and is her real brother...Since Jimmy Dean was gay, she can't have sex with her brother.*" These are stage directions of a sort, psychological, character setup, italicized. "Red," one of another stock of her personages, the "detective," talks in an "Age 16" section (chapter 11) of the manuscript named for her to one of her underworld, gang connections. This man is just beginning to look out for her on the streets. He says, "Shh, I'm not Harvey anymore. I'm Mommy." To contrast, *In Memoriam to Identity* of 1990, when seduction starts to go wrong: *'Do you want,' the French professor inquired, 'me to be your mommy?'*

6.

How old my author was when she died is up for debate. Writing in *The London Review of Books*, Gary Indiana puts her at 53, though this fact is just as coolly floated as is much of his take on Acker's work, development of her career, and supporters or detractors: *she had the cachet of a fetish object and did her best to look like one.* She wanted the "freedom that poetry enjoys over prose," but he faults her work, feeling: "Too often her novels were a barrage of attacks on writerly skills she lacked." In *The Blue Tape* film, made with poet Alan Sondheim, video footage I myself have seen, she provocatively, simply, slowly, caressingly, lovingly, plays with her breasts. In a memory of my viewing standing there with my notebook in the gallery, she is describing too what she is doing, how it is making her feel. What's done to me is not going to be done and gotten away with, without it having been re-marked upon by me. In Lynne Tillman's prose account, "Selective Memory," she recalls Acker "sitting on a table with her legs tucked under her. She's holding the microphone close to her mouth and she's whispering. She looks directly at the audience. She's referring to people and incidents some of the crowd know about. She's seductively hissing people's names into the mike that's now touching her lips." In the motion picture *The Golden Boat* (1990, music by John Zorn), Acker plays the part of a professor, rather than masturbator, and we travel up the wide stone steps of a columned building, to behind the door of a department of, I'm led to imagine, because of the letters cut from the frame, [An]thropolog[y], to where she sits, playing herself basically (same recognizable close-cropped hair, especially in those days for a woman, heavy flashes of silver earrings down and around the lobe, reddest of red lips, jeans) in a surprising context, a typewriter on the desk, a Jean Genet poster up on a file cabinet behind her in the background. We hear her ask the student who has come to see her, "Do you think you're going to continue in this manner?" Then begins a recited formula: if "x" is a killing of "y" by "z," then there is an "a" that is "y" or "y" is dying. And "x" is a causing of "a" by "z." We hear and she repeats. The bell rings, interrupting, for the next period. In the 1991 documentary film *Stigmata: The Transfigured Body*, Acker, flashing her gold tooth, discusses her piercings and her tattoos.

7.

No more keeping to forms easily recognized, no more business as usual. Mental processing resounds with compositional procedures. In a writing made of sex, reading, and dreaming, Acker makes to believe she is all sorts, brands, and types. Dreaming is a process she sees we could all stand to be more freely conscious of, as too often in the day-to-day one term will get set up over another: over forward thinking traditions, over the female the male, over the extreme a practical postulate. In *I Dreamt I Was a Nymphomaniac: Imagining*, collected as

8

part of her trilogy of identity works under the title *Portrait of an Eye*, a narrator decides, "For the new life, I have to change myself completely."

8.

In William S. Burroughs's compositional techniques, which Acker mimics initially, seeing in him the good-enough model, chance was to be sought and encouraged, random scissor slip privileged over along-dotted-lines premeditated excision. Burroughs's interests were in juxtaposition, the collage, the pieces arranged and superimposed over the flatter dimensions of grids, grinds, of a daily existence. That reader in run-of-the mill realism happy at home will read along lines of regulated frames of perception and feel everything is fine, clearly demarcating the inside from the outside, what is thought and what is done, and in the end everything fits all back together again somehow, whatever was purported to have been taken apart. Or there is chaos. In real life, things fall quite naturally into place too, don't they? Burroughs claimed what he wanted was non-dualistic systems. In her fictions, Acker would proceed to redress balances in society by investing heavily in, some ways camping out in, crisis points of the Other side. This is particularly true once her writing begins to consolidate itself along narrative lines to question and disrupt a nuclear family sown sacred locus for indoctrination into larger, societal versions of all those same seams. One should be wary, though, how on this "other" side there is for Acker no mother, capital M, or some other essentialist version of Woman. The attempt to come into her own is escaping in some ways from both of those functionaries as rarefied concepts and also troubling realities for her. In the literature, she would know the poor, the homeless, the starving, insane, the diseased, to generalize, the outcast, and not from a position of prescriptive measure, but rather as embodiments of lived experience. Her words she wants to disrupt as much as they might please. PORTRAIT: *Otherwise I don't exist: I'm a mirror for beauty.*

9.

Narratives start with our ages, our classes, our races, resources, hopes, matings, our nationalities, allegiances or no, and Acker's are no different. In the early work, *Kathy Goes to Haiti* (1978): "Kathy is a middle-class, though she has no money, American white girl, twenty-nine years of age, no lovers and no prospects of money, who doesn't believe in anyone or anything." To date the start of Acker's career—a "brilliant journey," as publisher Grove puts it in jacket copy for *Portrait of an Eye*—from 1973 has her writing in its earliest inception showing itself to be concerned fittingly with narratives of origin. Neatly, these early presentations had each other incarnations. The first two works of what has come to be known as her trilogy, *The Childlike Life of the Black Tarantula* and *I Dreamt I Was a Nymphomaniac: Imagining*, made up of six individual booklets each, initially existed as a parceled-out mail-art project reportedly sent to whomever wanted them, before they were all brought together. This business is often rehearsed in any Acker accounting, but gone over as well in the Lotringer interview. We might also set 1973 as our default departure point for Acker's journey if by that we mean a more organized publishing enterprise, the more sustained, concerted effort to get her work into the hands of others. In conversation with Ellen Friedman: "The first work I really showed anyone is *The Childlike Life of the Black Tarantula by the Black Tarantula*." A procedural term that extends beyond and begins before *The Childlike Life of the Black Tarantula*, "Tarantulas" is how she refers to "redoings." These are individual pieces based out of passages elsewhere. They are sketches, reinterpretations, or caricatures even if you like. In the fifth part of *The Childlike Life of the Black Tarantula*, she would become Yeats—the "I" of the text would—as at the same time "I explore my miserable childhood," to add to and complicate her own firsthand knowledge of herself, incorporating a lend of his autobiography. She made knowledge of selves sit down together and left a reader to try to reconcile. There then is a kind of freeze frame when another life or set of lives is picked up. Slices of experiences, lives, and the writings that come out of them become boxed-off, confined to individual "chapters." If anything runs through continuing pagination, it is an *I* of Acker behind a process she's documenting. We do not go back towards earlier threads to tie them in, to make them yet any part of some larger design: deranging her own sense of the *I* and the life she's living, where and how, while doing this, her work.

10.

Inside Acker's *The Childlike Life of the Black Tarantula by the Black Tarantula*, as with most of Acker's writing, a number of relations become formulated between self and other. Like in *The Burning Bombing of America*, "people are not only individual people." AMERICA: *your eyes are inside mine.* Possibly she starts with something like just as many eyes as the eponymous spider has at its disposal. You are told in *The Childlike Life* how "any person can become part of these composite insect eyes," in underscoring one of her rhetorical figures and strategies with which this choice work can be experienced evolving, the concept also become a string of strategic motifs that structure *The Childlike Life of the Black Tarantula* in the absence of stable characters along some steadily progressing plotted timeline. At times these motifs of the author as and author through spider become spider approximates, how constituting environment contributes to the caught intersections bled into each other, cat cradling.

11.

Identity is consolidated in this way, lines are drawn in desert or sea sand, and we may feel boxed in ourselves. One is trained in reading to try to perceive identity in a series of more or less stable relations between one "I" and its surrounding characters. Among the many categories she did not want to have her identity written off as: white woman. You are this one thing, before you are this other, you are told. Identity in Acker is in a tension with the reductive, what is seen, what is said. Another self-and-other dichotomy exists as that between the animal and human. AMERICA: *we no longer want to be human.* While she wants her work to be her world, she is also situating where one comes up against another. This body of mind, as much as any book page, in Acker is a modified subject site. In attempts ongoing to leave behind prior definitions and dominations, previous existences are there to be journeyed over and through to her own liking. These become complex, imaginative feed loops. "I always think that the more I learn, the wider the ocean in front of me becomes," she says in a letter to Richard Hell, his archive at Fales Library, too. I get a feeling this is not to be avoided but desired, the opening, expanding, this more to reach for and explore. Like a rabbit hole of her own, she tends to individual psyche: full of a plentitude of reflections, distortions, ruptures, and reroute potentials. AMERICA: *you know the world is your eyes.* AMERICA: *you are always your own home your love [ ] the child [ ] the mother [ ] and the father.* Imagination and desire, as they are sewn up by language especially, are contestable space found under almost constant bombardment in advancing visually saturated culture, where all dreams may be colonized already marketed back to us. The space in and around (recorded) language Acker wants to pry open, cut loose, opening queerly sights of mouths, legs, and minds. "Simone Weil," by Susan Sontag: *Perhaps there are certain ages which do not need truth as much as they need a deepening of the sense of reality, a widening of the imagination.* How the senses make that reality is one of the stakes for my subject. Acker works position self and writing at varied divides between public and private, ride these collapses, to challenge limiting and preconceived notions of decorum and form, to hope to express from what had been the repressed.

12.

The women that Acker picks as representative of sides of a self in her early piece, *The Childlike Life of the Black Tarantula by the Black Tarantula*, are born, have negotiations with their parents, and are then to marry men or get jobs. That was to be life. Desires though drive one towards other sensations, other mental pictures, and Acker from her start raises a fundamental, philosophical question: What keeps us separated from them? Stylistically, Acker's work would not confine itself to planes of reduction, frames of simple matters of what was true and what was false. Her portrait in *The Childlike Life* opens with an elucidating: "Intention: I become a murderess by repeating in words the lives of other murderesses." Acker wanted to dispense with bindings, their conventions, of gender, of genre, to overflow them, to make her own way more unlawfully embedded with others, their lives, their words, and by extension, make her own state more awe-filled. To point out this idea along developmental lines in her prose, Acker made exploration of the "I/eye" *regressing*. PORTRAIT: *I'm a child; I sense through touch.* I feel more than I see. Not yet do I know what is what. Where does the self, and where does memory, exist in such unscripting? PORTRAIT: *I look at my body as if it were a web, solely a way of asking people to touch me. My body doesn't exist.*

13.

In a tape of Acker interviewing him, Burroughs says of Brion Gysin, "He taught me to see a picture." We might say of Acker that, over her career, she too wants to keep teaching this herself to see differently. In *Rip-off Red*, this is the landscape the narrator is in: "The ceiling, floor, and walls of the winding hall are tiny mirrors placed against each other. I dance through this hall, twist my body into possible positions, and become a hundred kinds of criminals." Acker asks William Burroughs if there is any way for us to save ourselves, given the current state of the world, politics, she means. Burroughs questions who is meant by her us. Who is this "we"? Too often we see it taken for granted that everyone has the same givens in and on the books. Some of us want both and more. Some don't want to have to choose, one over the other, man over woman, the academic over experience, prose at an expense of our poetry, daddy over mommy. When no one man leads us no single form will hold us.

14.

Mais l'araignée de la haie / Ne mange que des violettes.... Where Rimbaud's spider in the hedge ("spinning," Paul Schmidt adds further in translation) is eating only violets, Acker will sit now in literature, among its blooms, and she would subsist through it. Anything to keep this world of a set coursing, from becoming too imprisoning this page.

15.

Comparable to a line in Acker's early novel attempt of *Rip-off Red*, "This is the story about how I have kept myself from being bored," another start in *I Dreamt I Was a Nymphomaniac*: "My name is Kathy Acker." Paragraph break. "This story begins by me being totally bored." In *Don Quixote* (1986), by Kathy Acker, it is the story of how one woman will achieve knighthood: "She had to name herself." The knighthood that is achieved when she "thought and acted as she wanted and decided" follows on the heels of the abortion opening the book, through which she makes a decision to love: "the most insane idea that any woman can think of." DON: *By loving another person, she would right every manner of political, social, and individual wrong: she would put herself in those situations so perilous the glory of her name would resound.* While some might define the aborting women all around our protagonist "bums" (ibid.), among whose numbers she may now count herself, the narrator reiterates, "She needed a new life. She had to be named." A wheelchair will be her steed, the "hack," and upon the terms she will be inclined, prompted to linguistically refract and reflect. The writer, in Acker's conception, is a bit of a workhorse. Two terms mirror meeting in a showdown, meaning. DON: *'once a hack' or 'always a hack' or 'a writer' or 'an attempt to have an identity that always fails.'* Early in this story, on the very first page, you have been told: *this's no world for idealism.* Acker refers to the world of the aborting character, held in bleak purview in these pages of her *Don Quixote,* become absorbing, too, an absurd relief: *she decided, 'catheter' is the glorification of 'Kathy.' By taking such a name which, being long, is male, she would be able to become a female-male or a night-knight.*

16.

"Age 11" (*Rip-off Red, Girl Detective*): "My mother tells me she hates my real childhood name, only gave me that name because she didn't think at the time it was legal right to give me my nickname. Her husband's sister who is crazy and whom she hates has my real name. She always calls me by my childhood nickname as does everyone I know: institutions at this time call me by my real childhood name." The childhood nickname I assume, Kathy, she keeps. In her earliest prose she endeavors to work through ideas of madness: not being able to hold onto the self in time, not being able to distinguish dream, fantasy, from reality, "nymphomania." She combines that childhood name with the surname, the taking of which arrives through marriage, a first. It removes Kathy-now-Acker from family graces. Born to money, she is disinherited. She claims, though not consistently, disinheritance is a result of whom she chose to marry. She sets her publishing, when she does forgo a fabrication of authorial pseudonyms, under these two signs. The tender protection of her childhood pet name, Kathy, abuts the one—Acker—making a mother's laws quite explicitly exclusionary. She did not marry within the class or up: down.

17.

In childhood, we play by deciding who we are going to be that day. For some of us, though, even here we do not find freedom unrestricted. At some point gender came in with its considerations. Consider, too, how somebody has to be the bad guy. Someone has to be the person to be captured and locked up. PUSSY, KING: *Prison. That's where Creon, my so-called dad, but he wasn't my real dad...wanted to put me.* These lines are spoken by a character of Antigone, designated "Antigone's Story," within a book that repeatedly reaches for and proceeds from climactic realizations. I enter ellipsis. Though the speaker is identified, the reader has been told in a flourish of bold italics that opens this story that this "Antigone" has also been called: *King Pussy, Pussycat, Ostracism, O, Ange.* "King Pussy's Story" and "Ostracism's Story" are included in a section of the book carrying a designation of "The Pirate Girls." Pussycat will be one of the characters subsequently related in Ostracism's story. O and Ange, on the other hand, have met each other in a whorehouse. It is by this point in Acker's career, towards the end, a repeating set. "In the Days of Dreaming," the last section is called. Antigone, again: *They put me inside 'cause I'm a girl. I've heard there are societies in which girls stay in prison until they're married. I'm out now so I'm never going to go back there.*

18.

In my subject, there will never be just one mirror, or only one reflection. You might abandon that hope, if ye enter here looking for only straight answers. No dream—language—of 1:1. She says it variously. In "Notes on Writing from the Life of Baudelaire": *All mental existence is expression, a measure of distance.* Untitled, incomplete manuscript (Papers): *One immediately comes up to language and learns either to be defeated or to let language fuck one, to fuck with language. To lie down. This is what I call 'fiction.'* "The Seattle Book": *I, I am proud here to announce to a world I don't at all know, I have never adjusted.* Agency will be conceived always as a shifting dialectic, a dialectic operating within her understanding of the self. PORTRAIT: *I look at myself in the mirror I don't understand whether I'm beautiful or plain or ugly I have to use what I see as an object make it as attractive as possible to other people. Now I'm two people.* The terms of the dialogue may shift from work to work and within the works, veering often midcourse, in contradistinction to more standard, straightforward reproductions of "realism," a term whose aptness, as a representational tool of our current social and psychic landscape in this modern world, is contested highly by Acker in an earliest alliance to William Burroughs and his authorial methods and aims. Acker points back in time repeatedly for precedent to him. Though put in quotes, "called 'The Female William Burroughs,'" the moniker is still opening lead in the publicity for the acquisition of the Kathy Acker

Papers by Duke University, the archive spanning 1972-1997. Classifications begin, even if self-elected. "I modeled my writing on him. I was 21! I'm 39 now. It's very old hat," she claims with McRobbie in the *Writers Talk: Ideas of Our Time* series, an extensive collection (106) of videos on Modern Literature and Philosophy for which Acker herself would eventually interview Burroughs (#52). Acker is #41, dated, when at all, 198_.

19.

Pondering what one might be left at liberty to imagine, she gives bodily quest the strongest allegorization in the female night: knight. Woman, like her *Don Quixote* character, could go mad or begin the making of her own myth, begin to try to illustrate her own reality or as she would want to have it lived. PORTRAIT: *I'm simply exploring other ways of dealing with events than ways my lousy habits—mainly installed by parents and institutions—have forced me to act.* In her last novel, *Pussy, King of the Pirates* (1996), Acker pries the caste of Robert Louis Stevenson's *Treasure Island* open, and inserts girls right there along with the pirates, girls now too, working through her writing anarchic plundering, re-figuring, re-sourcing *goods*: planting girls everywhere. Literary heresy, perhaps, and textual sorcery is not to be dismissed. I see riffs here pushing off of the theorization of Catherine Clément, those contributions to her co-authored book with Cixous, 1975's *The Newly Born Woman*. You find yourself deeply in the heart of a maze, in the center of which can be seen sitting trapped, above all else, the woman in the place of the repressed and monstrous. Acker maps dreams out. Dreams tattoo imagination, and with her tattoos, Acker maps her body. Acker draws out id that has been consolidated into identity through proffered routes of cosmetic, consumerist society. Drawings of dreams become one of the fabrics of her books' narratives, as she believes these might lead to treasures for herself or at least for her characters, or she is told that, if she just figures how to see them best.

20.

Once she begins, she will not cease looking for ways out, more paths to foray in more ways to supplement old logics. Burroughs's prior experimental methods of the fold-in and the cut-up, sampling just two in his arsenal, were queer. He made these not alone but together with another man, Gysin. They do not pretend to some natural procreation. To accounting of the divine and blind inspiration, she leverages understandings gleaned through taking stock of prior experiences, the existences and orientations of her materials. Acker explains in "A Few Notes on Two of My Books": *you can make, but you don't create.* Acker will utilize what already exists in the world around her, bringing the techniques of other mediums to bear on her life and writing. Everything is already in the world—you are pulling always from the other glosses, separating yourself from what already is. Rather than giving rise to, she transposes the techniques of filmmaking into her writing. For example, montage, and as she says too in a moment of addressing with Lotringer her process, "the harder the cut the better." One aim is to play around with changing speeds of developments. Such has effects on comfort zones of readers. Acker says with McRobbie how Charles Olson said, stressing, "To write about something is academic, and to *do* it in your writing is visceral." She dispels any claim of being the first or last word on any subject. What Acker does here is to take a bit of Olson's authorization to grant her own.

21.

In Acker's collection of essays, *Bodies of Work* (1997), outside the confines of the 1990 essay devoted to him, "William Burroughs's Realism," Burroughs makes some other notable appearances. In "A Few Notes on Two of My Books," she praises the "immediacy," in contradistinction to *most of the writing in the contemporary novels of this country.* A preceding sentence, "Living in England, I keep returning to American literature," keeps that country's antecedent unclear. She places Burroughs within a list she says Sade would head for her. Dropping in Sade's name is also how Acker begins in the particular essay to sidestep a purely American-English context in establishing precedent for her writing, along with Burroughs, a movement she continues to work on as the essay is progressing. *'Marginal,' 'experimental,' and 'avant-garde' are often words used to describe texts in this other tradition. Not because writing such as Burroughs's or Genet's is marginal, but because our society, through the voice of its literary society, cannot bear immediacy, the truth, especially the political truth.* They provide an alternative line of what one might pursue, how much further one might go. In Burroughs, the word, the sentence, punctuation, of life regulated is a control both acquired and imposed. A frame of consciousness might be moved out, out. Long lines of prior breakthroughs documented would be there to be uncovered and re-spun to legend purpose anew. Everything is permitted, Burroughs would have you know, Hassan i Sabbah founder of the Assassins quoted saying, last words on a deathbed. Through prophesy in his *Illuminations*, Rimbaud commands: *Behold an age of* Assassins ("Drunken Morning"), sentiment Acker makes in one of her *In Memoriam to Identity* translations read as, "Now is the time for murder." She takes in the adaptation, as she would in multifarious ways in her work, liberty.

22.

Mirrors and walls are granted a metaphorical agency to conspire together. PORTRAIT: *I'm a mirror.* Also in the same work: *presenting a wall of shivering to anyone who tries to talk to me.* I'm not so solely two-dimensional, as I'm not quite so deferential. Symbols conflate and collide, to join forces to corner the subject, overturn as they trade-off among each other no clear lines between their "selves," objecthood, maintained. Acker pushes points, as her tension is built in anticipation of the rhetorical crisis then executed. Her metaphors become narratively self-reflexive. PORTRAIT: *The walls are going to close around me: crush me....* Acker shows herself to have many selves subjected inside her. PORTRAIT: *The walls are the legs of a huge spider.* Her object of inquiry is shown to be subject to change. This figuring of further understandings, "consciousnesses," in loops of relays keep giving and contributing to more troubled understanding of any "main" ever character her work displays. For as many "selves" as she has begun to ink in exist as many more complements to possibly take off from. This has implications for how multiply something like love might be conceived, optimistically. A form of wager of a multi-faceted nature can be seen set down in the early (predating *The Childlike Life of the Black Tarantula*)

22

"Journal / Black Cats [ ] Black Jewels," a path of connections
that need not be restrictive: *I love L. M. W. M. B. H. (L.)?*

23.

Let yourself come out, let yourself mingle with the other "I"s
on the page. Wonder: who is ever going to be able to tell the
difference, where you begin and end. Wonder if there will
be a point where not even you can any longer see supposed
differences between you and others, even those society makes
its profit through demonizing. These accounts she could try to
turn into her own, by herself slipping into them, trying to take
more account of herself from their vantage. The I-doubled,
at least, the one that concedes it does and will see through
others, the "I" that does not try to hide it relies in part upon
the identities of others for its own, could this I be seen to be a
viable alternative for proceedings? Much narration in her work
exists in the premise of this "I" in flux. To come at herself from
variable ends, Acker calls out across a page. Wrong becomes
relative in her explorations, the movement of the writing in
its goals, how stringently it directs itself, how efficiently, how
virulently. She would make literature by writing the dreams of
fantasy, believing they held not the keys to her correction, but
expanding of consciousness, un-single-filing. PORTRAIT: *I
began to separate myself: to watch the violence of my desires
more and more.* Born rich, to dispense with identity traps you
might choose not to stay entitled, might attempt to slough off
the old set, the routine. There is a slight shift of designation
when her work "Implosion" is folded into the book named
My Death My Life by Pier Paolo Pasolini. A scene title, "The
Punk World," becomes dedication: *For the Punk World.*

The last thirteen lines of the earlier version are reset as "My Grandmother's Memory" (a convict tells her, "Remember, child, remember.") *Great Expectations* (1982), "Any action no matter how off-the-wall—this explains punk—breaks through deadness."

24.

Disruption at the level of the sentence is true of much early, unpublished work found in her Papers, like "Journal / Black Cats [ ] Black Jewels," with its capitalizing of only single letters to designate characters (*B. becomes B. B. melts into B. I am anarchy*), with its irregular periods and holes of [white] space (*who am I [ ] echo [ ] who am I*) cut through pieces of sentences: "I forget all recent developments" (*accept what emotion appears*). In the text "Entrance Into / Dwelling In / Paradise," the introduction of a fade of meaning into the unit of the sentence is brought home into the enclosing word, "gar den," and the idea of succinct closure, a concluding sentence, becomes jimmied through, too, this disruption set down visually to the field of the page: she has a final sentence repeatedly backing up on itself, a cluster of type that runs more and more into itself toward the edge of the border, further down it falls, words more and more impossible to separate out from the sentence above, developing an impasto almost but for the medium. Both of these works are dated 1972, as is "Homage to Leroi Jones," privately published by the Abort Gold Press. It is not only the mark of Burroughs's influence: these words of violences of technologies, often rooted in cities, run through and re-constructing subjects, considered and seen considered by Acker in interviews and writings on her, on both levels of content and form. But they also seem to exhibit to degrees those coded auto/biographies some use as a way in for the reading of Gertrude Stein.

25.

Though it is only one prison, gender is tied into other personality lockdowns, for example, domestic servitude. It is with as much seeming relief as loss for a direction that a wandering *I* of that early, foundational *Childlike Life of the Black Tarantula* announces: "I'm not sure whether I'm a male or a female." PORTRAIT: *I'm not sure what I am.* Gender indeterminacy, as explored in Acker, is as much a blessing, an escape, and departure point, as any hindrance. Like the "Antigone" of *Pussy, King*, the "I" of Acker's *Don Quixote* is also promiscuous rover, in senses both as a character and signification, and punished by a mother's taunts. DON: *'You've come to prison of your own free accord,' my mother barked when I returned from the bathroom.* It is where "I" has run to cry, to try to escape her parents' voices, after returning home from a disastrous attempt at self-expression in New York. DON: *I didn't feel normal in a normal household and, wanting to be me, I wanted to express me.* That trip ended with the need to, "suck cocks while their owners held guns to my head" and go "running after men who might protect me." *Love was rape and rejection*, and: *My only reaction to continuous devaluation was autism.* Unlike Antigone, who has vowed to never return, this "I" has come back to the mother character, one going on to assert: *The family is the only refuge any of us has.* Right on the heels: *'You're my property,' daddy amended. 'From now on, you will do whatever I woof you to do and,*

more important, be whoever I order you. This is a safe unit.'
If the daughter will only learn to comply, if she will concede
to folding herself back safely inside commands of previously
established structures, Dad the barker will protect her, from
herself, from that outside world, both of which he claims. In
Acker's flush stories, characters like this "I" will function to
not only show, but see also, lawful identities as conjunctions of
sex and place, cages, in society. *I should learn to stay under the
wing of the, his, house.*

26.

To have the reader making swings forward like jump cuts and
reattachments, Acker's work repeatedly sections itself off. As
one must navigate the chasms of reassurance through their own
devices, you become more fluid in them. You might lay down
identity props for a moment. The tale through time spins in
a web of perspectives. A metaphor by now having acquired
its own dimensions and history, reading aspects the spider
brings with it back into Acker's work is not a move I pretend
to originate with me. In "Confessions of a Kleptoparasite,"
Martina Sciolino does it, the kleptoparasite a bird, insect, or
other animal that habitually robs those of other species of
food, as Acker's writing may be said crucially to do with other
authors' offerings. It is of a perfect piece. Quite elegantly, in
both the thinking and design, Juliana Spahr lyrically explores
the fits between criticism itself and the words of others it needs
to continue in survival, fruitfully, in her essay *Spiderwasp*.
Acker's structure accretes rather than restricts. It continues
to add to itself, multiplying its senses of self, never trapped
behind just one function, never too framed—walled in—or too

immobilized for too long. PORTRAIT: *I sit against the white walls of the enclosed room and gibber. The walls are all white. The walls of an asylum. The walls of a hospital.* New eyes to see through could offer new outs, techniques she pulls from a wide range of cultural schools and artistic fields. Changing *I* mid-stream, paragraph, page or chapter in the process of the book, before our very own eyes, Acker prompts those initial orientations to crumble, seen as tenuous, unconsolidating losses, scrambling one forward in leaps of faith or knots we make in going on. There is deferring, or one needs to know now. As Susan Howe in *My Emily Dickinson* takes issue with Gilbert and Gubar, confronting her heroine in *The Madwoman in the Attic* with prescriptive, reductive approach for the sake of thematic coherence, I find a struggle not only between covers, but also across my subject's writings against short-sighted synthesis, for the sake of more unequivocal, more impressive perhaps arguments. In her interview with Larry McCaffery, "The Path of Abjection," collected in *Some Other Frequency*, Acker: "I love Sade's work because you can argue endlessly and no fucking person agrees. You can go through Klossowski, de Beauvoir's, all the essays on him, and *nobody*—Bataille, Sarduy, anybody—can reach any agreement whatsoever. It's magnificent!" This writing reflects to me what appealed to her about that of Sade.

27.

No matter how apparently autobiographical the incident related, how easily conflated with what we believe we know of the facts of this author's actual life, she was particularly interested in trying on the lives of friends: boyfriends and writers, artists, coworkers. As she tries to see how well they might fit her own thoughts, Acker would tailor them to her own ends. On the surface level it is very rarely seamlessly. Though these other lives could be confused at times for her own, might not be all her own, something like a life in theory emerges over her work. There is a withdrawn, though overshadowing and controlling mother, who wanted to abort her, who will suicide one day if she has not already. There is an abusive, sexually more often than not, dad, not really her biological father. This overview of some of the strides she would eventually hit and loop would not be complete if we were not to include stripping, its routines and its relation to other facets of life, a veritable aesthetic.

28.

All that separates the dream, the vision, "fiction" from *reality* on the page is arrangement of the words, classified or not and how, a line separating in the world or in the head. At times in the *Childlike* work, Acker will deign to tell us when we've just had what. "Fourth fantasy," for example. Acker is writing with a beginning proposition. Put two different **I**'s on a page side by side. Then put yourself in a parenthesis among them. Then go ahead. Put more. "I" begins to live by reading and repeating among the at times confusing overlaps with words, their marked degrees of characterization or unmarked (some murderesses, "moll cutpurse, the queen-regent of misrule, the roaring girl, the benevolent tyrant of city thieves and city murderers, the bear lady"). "I" exists in close proximity in fantasy to "Helen Seferis" used by Acker as not primarily masturbatory material, but also as a means of creating further writing. All she need do is set it down, what comes up in her as she reads. As much as Acker identifies with this character in Scottish "beat" and junkie Alexander Trocchi's *Helen and Desire*, Acker identifies with the creator, the crafting seduction of intrigue underhanded. One convention mediates the very pretense of "Helen," her character. These pages you are now given to read, or so the setup goes, you are being led to believe are in actuality her journal, the narrative as "found," only slight edits and interjections, and consequently, unfortunately, there are some stretches missing... By writing the lives, and holding her own up to them, setting down alongside it and through it, intercutting the histories, further lives and characters and myths taken up, Acker through the work of the book stages folding events from her frame of own time onto other philosophical points, the two becoming indistinguishable, to her even, even Sade, kink in the father machine.

29.

EXPECTATIONS: "Daddy, you don't even know who Dostoyevsky is." The father figure in Acker is variously a drunk or just dumb, someone wanted or drawn as rapist. In both *Rip-off Red* and *The Childlike Life of the Black Tarantula*: "My father tries to rape me." PORTRAIT: *My father wants to fuck me, fears his desire which is the only honest part of him, and fears me.* It is written as the father's third heart attack that hospitalizes him in the opening of "Requiem" (1997). In an early, unpublished short piece not to be confused with her novel of the same name, *Blood and Guts in High School*, bearing little to no resemblance but for the protagonist called in both "Janey," the father is dying in a hospital after his fifth heart attack. Then we cut from there to a poem:

One day he came suddenly back to the winter
Apartment in the summer
And caught a boy's tie in the bathtub
He started to cry and told me
I shouldn't go with any other men but him
He began to rub

My breast he told me
No other man could give me
Security
But him.

The detail of the tie gets often upgraded in other Acker fiction to being caught in the midst actually of the act of fucking in the bathtub. I want to present too how the role of a father plays into a stretch in her *Great Expectations*. Towards the middle of a paragraph column within which things are speeded-up with commas taking the place of periods, letting us get a quick breath but not full-stop, before the next unit of meaning hits the *father* we opened with grabbing a candle cuts quickly to *soldier* taking out his knife and the writer fumbling for a right word for his *sex*, trying to capture that and get it pinned down (*his pincher his grabber*) as scenes in the paragraph come together and words "raping" and "rape" are used before: *I walked into my parents' bedroom opened their bedroom door don't know why I did it, my father was standing naked over the toilet, I've never seen him naked I'm shocked, he slams the door in my face, I'm curious I see my mother naked all the time....* The narration then in one sentence still only marked off as any sort of containment unto itself by a preceding comma—rather than period—still just pause and not full-stop, no more of a marked

30

distinction in time, tells a story that grows in complications. A mother "closely watches"—the daughter, it can be inferred or assumed from this point on, before the next word, *inside*, seems to cue to shift the reader in some retreat back into that soldier father fantasy story dreamed as read earlier. The subsequent tone, though, experiences modulation. Now *the young girl* throws a hand of her own into the coupling in the book and "sucks out of the curly brownhaired's cheeks the black meat." At the same time as neighboring dogs escape cages, there is thought: *treat me like a dog.*

30.

I don't create the metaphors I work with: one book will become one frame, as one chapter may, one character, just as one "I." PORTRAIT: *I can see anything in a set of shifting frameworks.* PORTRAIT: *I see a frame around me: my space.* Acker records the fantasies she is able to conjure from others' acts, authorships and their books. Other books become not ends, not final words, but what can be known as transitional objects. As do become other authors, artists, be they poets, critics even, theorists for her own books, even within the pages of her own books.

31.

"Seeing Gender": *I couldn't even run away to sea like Herman Melville.* In the "Wedekind's Words" writing that comprises part of the second division of Acker's *Don Quixote*, she tries to translate her version onto and through another. She tries to give doomed "Lulu" a makeover in a new adventure, a new destiny. Lulu speaks, "As soon as I reached the ground, I ran to the sea." "Now I must find others who are, like me, pirates journeying from place to place, who knowing only change and the true responsibilities that come from such knowing sing to and with each other." And, "Now I am going to travel." Traveling, journeying, becomes one of the keys, come back to time and again, in our movements through Acker. She makes a trope of it. As early as *The Burning Bombing of America*: "this is a map for future journeys." *Pussy, King of the Pirates* concludes with an actual map as a page of endpaper.

32.

The romance with literature becomes a myth about herself Acker will make preserved the way she wants. Such a reliance on literature to hold one's self is given documentation in the "Seeing Gender" essay, one of her last (1995). *...I ran into the world of books, the only living world I, a girl, could find. / I never left that world.* Here the narrator constructs an understanding she locates in her "childhood," as this section of the essay is named. *I couldn't murder my parents because I couldn't imagine murdering them.* Someone like Electra, however, could, and she would call upon her brother for help in the department. *Brothers* are the men she can trust. In the "Seeing Gender" essay, Acker would also posit the pirates—who don't have parents, she tells us, so don't imagine having to murder them—who live in books where she finds them, in distinction to the dead world of decorum that is assigned to parents: "my bossy mother and my weak father," "a man who isn't mean enough to her, who yields to her every silly whim."

33.

It is within *The Childlike Life of the Black Tarantula* that gender confusion is first overtly introduced into her work. The once knit-up threads of a fragile proving web are no longer held so assuredly—in characters that do or don't serve our identifications—as the author elect feeds upon and generates their alternate identities and ends. PORTRAIT: *Of course, I disguise myself as a man.* This also marks the first real modification with far-reaching implications of Burroughs's concerns. Imagine him imaging himself a woman, feeling that his mobility, word, might be liberated, increased, by such. Imagine a time when racist language was just part of what he did, if he did it broadly enough. He is a veritable hero for some. Some parts are just forgotten. PORTRAIT: *When I wear tight pants, I watch my cock rise and fall it looks like a small animal only I know it's me....* The narrator, imagining, believes: *A cock feels like, it feels like me, I can sense it hang outward from my body sort of down, I don't really feel anything though I know it's there, I feel proud: a piece of flesh.* The narrative evolves, through such an attempt to see, a reconstructed vision of a self, newly "thick skin" with "tender low breasts with huge violet nipples the skin below them curves downward over man's hips to heavy long spider's legs."

34.

An environment that informs and delimits is constructed around one's "I." Within this environment, creating spaces for herself, framing, wrapping around herself through other portraits in words, Acker plays with an image. The spider can make its home wherever it goes. Writing is a web too of the materials. Undoing the determining marks of gender, toward neutrality English can take with its animals and objects, all but our human, becomes an action illustrated in Richard Howard's translation of Roland Barthes's "Théorie" fragment in his *Pleasure of the Text*. You can watch how writing, in its metaphorical move not confined to "female," can enjoy the erotic slip of a gendered restraint: "the subject unmakes **himself**, like a spider dissolving in the constructive secretions of **its** web." My emboldening. Indeed, though, the male tarantula does spin, too: a sperm web is a mat of threads made, rubbed up against, to provoke secretion and hold its release. They burrow in two ways: *obligate*, making their own holes, or, retreating into hollows already there: "opportunistic." All tarantulas are cannibalistic, though most kept pets, for gentle natures, are female.

35.

Some details—with the appearance of autobiography—manifest themselves over and over again in the work around how we feel living. They create an intimacy, for those who go further through the books, of a narrating history: linchpins. We might see these as instances of the "biographemes," perhaps even fabricated to degrees, that Roland Barthes makes a call for in his *Sade/Fourier/Loyola*. In Acker's case, she selects them herself. When she interviews Juan Goytisolo: "I just wanted you to talk a little about your relationship with some of the French theory, like Roland Barthes." Goytisolo answers, "Roland Barthes went on the theory and myself I made the practice of the theory." The transcript is in her papers. These are a few of those things Acker won't or can't through her books forget. These gambits become definitional: how our authorial site can be said to be not just like the rest, in all the different book identities she might try on. Measures of relief—hers, mine, structurally—emerge, as do names I begin to follow through her. These biographemes in her nature lay the bedrock psychology of protagonists and arguments, providing connective arches through and across her word landscapes, lending what Wittgenstein (I've seen Acker be aware of him, too) might call the *family resemblance* between many of the figures characteristic of her output. Here is what she would like to believe, what she would like us to know, what she needs in order to ground the fictions, other writings. They are the details through which she invests in the texts. These become blocks of memories. These are the things you must learn to play with in the creative enterprises, expressive often in the essays as well. Acker herself suggests a metaphor for the processing: *like playing with building blocks*, to Lotringer she says. Squaring off and isolating segments of the original to move those around, building upon and through articulating them, and she will use the building blocks comparison again—repeat another—elsewhere. She tells a reporter for the local periodical in some outpost where she is hired gun for a college to attend to aspiring writers (*The Argonaut*, in her Papers): a child plays with them. "My great joy was to take things, put them together, take them apart, see how they worked."

36.

One of the walls one of the narrators of *The Childlike Life of the Black Tarantula* at loss for direction is up against is being alone in the apartment: *The windows are two huge eyes staring at me.* The motif of the windows as eyes to find a way out through structurally underpins, even when not more metaphorically invoked as *mise en scène*. In *Great Expectations*, she adds to the complex of her compositional endeavor, when for example Acker brings the "I" up against Proust's, dramatizing how she subsequently incorporates sentences and pages of his into her own. Once she begins to look through his "window," once absorbed in Proust's language, the reader sees the narrator no longer alone in the book (we are reading, and the book the narrator is reading has its own narrator, of course, too...) in the very moment ours slides away from us to be held through another. Proust is chosen for a porousness she goes through, the vision of plenty Acker appropriates for her placement, in taking up his tale— not a crushing empty accusing space of that earlier *Childlike* narrator's environment at home. Proust's language becomes privileged along the narrator's own material lines: *The only reason, at bottom, why I enjoyed looking at Proust's words was because I said to myself, 'It's pleasant to have so much verdure at my bedroom window,' until suddenly*—and here comes the glad meeting of an I-to-I taking place in the richness of a perspective shift, after a comma above, for "in the vast, verdant picture I recognized—but brushed by contrast in deep blue simply because it was farther away—the spire of the church at Combray," "not a representation of that spire, but the spire itself, which, bringing thus before my eyes distance in both space and time, had come and outlined itself on my windowpane in the midst of the given foliage but in a very different tone, so dark that it almost seemed as if it had been merely sketched in." This environment, clipped and pruned as it may be, the break or two I do to try to more cleanly parse:

it begins to live inside Acker's own *Great Expectations*; in miniature her narrator taken into the narration of discerning Proust. Words whet in anticipation of admiring the images from afar before leaping forward, floating then off further into his landscape, shifting shared direction. When through that connection of a comma joining, joint of guide in a hand, he lives inside her "I." An absorbing reading experience is created along with the narrator to have, one of integration into that which emanates.

37.

Acker mentions many figures of her current moment, in her works, as well as more safely valued and more secure ones. These figures may or may not help her out along the way, but she begins playing them together to see. LECTER: "I was introduced to Robert Kelly and Jackson Mac Low and to the work of Charles Olson. So you might say I had an early training in Black Mountain School rhetoric.... I must have been very influenced by them, but certainly in a perverse way. Charles Olson said that when you write what you have to do is find your own voice, but it all seemed to be very big, almost God-like, and I found this very confusing. I couldn't find my own voice, I didn't know what my own voice was." I elide a bit. Elsewhere, in another rehearsal of the story of origins, in a manuscript in her Papers, Acker remembers her man differently, "I remember that someone, was it Robert Creeley? said that you become a poet when you find your own voice. I remember that I couldn't find my own voice: I knew very well what I couldn't stand and whom. Pretty much the whole world which my family, school, and society had given me and tried to make me into. I was in revolt...above all, revolt against myself, the person everyone seemed to want me to be. A nice, pretty girl who never made any fuss and married well." Though some might be taken aback, Creeley is right there on the back of the Grove edition of the *Great Expectations* book, lending his voice. "The novel's remarkable investment of hackneyed originals makes a prose of shimmering precision. Words, ideas, and the concepts that engender them come together in a singularly echoing tour de force of one woman's life, like they say, in the many places where imagination has heretofore proposed it to be." Or, in other words, this time those of Rimbaud we might adopt, whom Acker cites, holds up, and can often be seen to also paraphrase: *I shall never have any hand!* As laid out in one of the poems that opens and orients ("Bad Blood") his *A Season in Hell*, the loss of a hand is for Rimbaud not accepting a "proper" use for one. Revolting prodigy, he is formulating his back turned on what he calls "domesticity," *la domesticité*. Before an angry mob, Rimbaud exclaims himself *comme* Joan of Arc, she of the shaved head Acker would also relate to visually. PORTRAIT: *I cut off my hair; I'm Joan of Arc. I lead soldiers in drag and kill everyone.* "She was the first woman in San Francisco to regularly wear a crewcut," Ron Silliman says in speaking of her. We are so many years away from Ms. Spears staring out onto a futuristic, devastated cityscape, singing like a protégé of musician mastermind Prince ("I'm A Slave 4 U") before losing her mind and shaving *hers*. In *Politics*, Acker writes, "I'm in the bathtub touching the bones in my face I have no idea what I feel like...I want to shave my hair off again...I admire criminals in my head knowing they're shits businessmen motherfuckers like everyone else...."

38.

There was a state for her that would go on and would continue to structure itself through different memories or different crisis points in all of Acker's major fiction in one way or another, and it would be made also to underpin variously essays and her understandings in non-fiction. In writing on New York City, and her connection to it, in a manuscript draft, she breaks her experiences into two childhoods. She recalls a playing of pirate, trawling the streets of juvenescence (*My love for New York, being the love for one's place of birth or one's birth, will die only when I do*), and she calls this her first childhood. Her *second childhood*, according to her, would begin when she became an adult. This is a development that she locates in the *underground*—the artistic center of which she tells us was NYC. It was shortly after the coup of a 1981 Pushcart Prize awarded to "New York City in 1979," produced for Acker by Anne Turyn's publishing venture *Top Stories*, that Acker made it to the larger houses.

39.

Though they are more evolved and more sustained, and thus become more involved than earlier Acker exercises, the ends underpinning the projects of *The Childlike Life* and the *Nymphomaniac: Imagining* initially are not to be novels, postmodern or otherwise—though given that eventual designation when collected as part of *Portrait of an Eye: Three Novels*. Publication under a rubric does push a point and create a slightly different interpretational frame for reading the works. Now they are read in light of other novels, how others work. If 1973 begins a journey for Kathy Acker, it may be that it is towards the regulated, increased composing by her of texts that might later more easily be classified, collected and called novels. These first saved pieces she begins to refer to as her trilogy.

40.

In notes for an early and, at least in this form, apparently abandoned project, a translation of *The Thesmophoriazusae* by Aristophanes taken up in the stead of a proposed earlier translation of *Lysistrata*, she knows already, "I don't want my writing even my translating to be an act that occurs apart from the other acts of my life." And also as part of these notes in her Papers: "If I follow my hates, I don't turn myself into a robot-tyrant so that I can get a job only way I can earn money which buys food and shelter, I have to depend on my brother's slave labor working at a porno-shop two dollars an hour. Pain." The making of the always new novel distraction to spring up disconnected from all else, piercing to no heart of no already existing matters, or Acker wants to use what's already around her. She would take the influence, and she would try running with this. Acker takes a "novel" as a form to invent along with and through, comparable to her expressed plans for translating the play. "Obviously even with translation of words of play there'll be collage-style diary accounts intervening." And in her own defense: "I'm sure these concepts are weird and unethical, but I'm weird too." The authoring procedure that she moves into that would become hers fights against meaning-making in pro-creating the "naturalness" of Godhead-given, granted, and situated where it has been and recognized thus far. In correspondence over her Tarantula productions, she expresses a fear of being stuck in a diary, though she will never completely leave the diary behind. It remains, albeit incorporated, within her surrounding fictions, providing relief from the more solitary in her mind, confines of a practice that can be debased. An essay by Chris Kraus, "Shit On My Sleepmask," illuminates a bit in formulating, "diary-keeping is not a popular art. It sounds too much like something girls do. *Theories* of subjectivity sounds sexier and more important. Since diary-writing is subjective practice, it's more fragile, looser, messier. As a transcription of live thought, diary-writing's destined for confusion because the mind does not stay still for very long. As an art-making-practice, it's incoherent and therefore essentially flawed." Her emphasis on theories. Two dates run through *The Childlike Life of the Black Tarantula*, one that appears to be the date of the composing (transcribing, coping, or transposing) and those dates in sources the lives are being lifted from. The fourth section of this work evinces a more daily dating, e.g. 7/18; 7/20/73; 7/21; 7/22, etc. By the end of this piece, Acker has brought herself up to the point of trying to identify the self with, through, two authors, male ones, who created works as well as sources of colorful biographies (Yeats, Sade). One thing Acker does in this *Childlike* and early work is not hide the process that goes into it but rather inscribe it as part of it, amp it. She does not ever really leave behind the poetry, either.

41.

Blood and Guts in High School: "Since she had no idea how to write poetry, she copied down all she could remember every pukey bit by the Latin poet Sextus Propertius which she had been forced to translate in high school." Peter Guttridge's obituary for Acker in the London *Independent* tells how "she had fallen in love with Latin at school, particularly the poets Catullus and Propertius." Sextus himself as a character is introduced in the third section, called "The End," of Acker's *Great Expectations*, in a timeline entry for 29 B.C.: *Empire begins. Centralization of power which is thought. Any non-political action such as poetry goes against centralization. Ovid is expelled. Propertius and Horace are told they have to write praises of the empire. Expulsion.* Worked out of the praise of society. With slight alteration and one rearrangement, the majority of "The End" section becomes five scenes making up "Act Two" of Acker's play "The Birth of the Poet." Hardin in his Acker introduction: "Her poetry is the most difficult to track down, since much of it was published in tiny journals in the late 60s and 70s that are no longer in print." The year of the composition if not release of her work "Politics," 1968, is also listed as the date of the publication of four poems by her, *Untitled*: "there is a dream of love," "your checks are pale," "you lie there against the sheets," "you watch me pressing my breasts."

42.

Perhaps just as strong as Acker's fear of being stuck in a diary, coeval with that fear, was a desire to not find her work limited or relegated only to a close-knit circle of poet friends. In all-caps, in one of the more manifesto-like stretches of the highly urgent, angry, and beautifully scattered *The Burning Bombing of America*: ST. MARK'S CHURCH IS A REVOLUTIONARY CRUISE-JOINT. In the short piece

"Lust," Dick is a poet who makes his home there in that location. He "hated feelings and cunts," and his creed was "poetry is more powerful than politics." The walls of such poetry as the world are ready to close in around. This is not a crowd she would want to blend into or fit in with. Poetry would be no sanctuary outside of the polis if delimiting appropriate bodies from which it might issue. Though the turns of many of her sentences are themselves as lines poetic, even when Acker doesn't feel the need to announce and segregate them as such, what gives the lines voice is the body dramatized they issue from. What keeps these voices from being just speakers, just mouthpieces? An answer is a body politic they interact with, within which and around which she tracks. Poems are still all the time being smuggled, more or less covertly, into her books of novels. She creates a haven of her own, harboring, while all the while identifying with whatever comes from what others call the bottom or below. In *Empire of the Senseless*, in a near-future vision of a dystopian Paris rocked by successful revolution: opening the map and into a flourishing of changing characters, partners persist, as Acker keeps practicing the vocal expansion of interiors around and through them. EMPIRE: *'All I know is that we have to reach this construct. And her name's Kathy.'* I think of my favorite Alice Notley collection, *Alice Ordered Me to Be Made*, 1975 poems. How the pieces come into place for our understanding of her is how Kathy will be made. A poem, in a section of the book called an "elegy," assigns the heart a country and is followed by prose that proclaims: *The only thing I desire is innocence.* Pieces are broken down along a numbered list. *Is there any other knowing besides this remembering?*

"How Spring Came to the Land of Snow and Icicles" is from *Blood and Guts in High School*, a note accompanying excerption credits. When published alone it is illustrated with drawings both cartoonlike and surreal in their anthropomorphisms: a beaver or bear in a hat, full-page, corpulent dinosaur naked but for stilettos, pearls, and makeup. "You get published how you get published," Acker says in the video interview with cultural critic Angela McRobbie, in response to critical reception as a "punk" or "Downtown" writer. A performance artist called "Colette" in *The Poets Encyclopedia* is there as an explorer of fashion and female persona. Acker was not then alone in multifarious, overlapping fields of enquiry, as Colette does an entry for "Justine" (Sade). Acker sees what she is doing, and what she desires to do, in conceptual terms. As related at the end of one of the sections making up *The Childlike Life of the Black Tarantula*, "All of the above events taken from *The Marquis de Sade The Complete Justine Philosophy in the Bedroom and Other Writings* by Count Donatien Alphonse Francois de Sade, *Portrait of de Sade* by W. Lenning, and myself." She is at one point in that milieu of the St. Mark's Poetry Project, named by Peter Wollen "her first port of call" and also "quickly abandoned." He notes this in his primer essay, collected in *Lust for Life: On the Writings of Kathy Acker*, initially in the London Review of Books as "Don't Be Afraid to Copy It Out," and more (Barbara Kruger thinks she's not positive enough). "Even the poets at St. Mark's, considered an avant-garde mecca for Modernists, were baffled by her approach to writing." To Lotringer, Acker offers, "Sol Lewitt subsidized me, that's what happened." It can also be argued she worked through the emerging scene of Language poetry, before she was "token maverick" more in the mainstream, as Acker understands it. Executor Matias is somewhat in opposition to me here: "...a few writers I know...are determined to have K spun as someone who works in the tradition of and in dialogue with the Language poets. Now that's a hard one; I just can't see it." There is a description of a given lecture in *My Mother: Demonology*, where "Language Poets" are at stake. Viegener generously goes on: "But I would never impede them from writing anything, and would in fact help them if they needed permissions, bibliography (& certainly opinions!)." I see Acker believing she might move on to the less cloistered. Ron Silliman gives this account of the early author and her means of distributing her writing. Monday, December 05, 2005, Silliman's Blog: "Once each month she would hand me these self-printed chapters from her ongoing work in progress.... Publishing chapters monthly, handing them out to friends, struck me as deeply romantic, going right back to Dickens as a model for the form, yet also extraordinarily brave. [...] The courage of Acker's actions was an important impetus to me...." Six booklets or discrete publications come together to form the whole of each *The Childlike Life of The Black Tarantula* and *I Dreamt I Was a Nymphomaniac!* The eventual republication and collection omits the exclamation point. Where Silliman uses the term "chapters," the individual sections by Acker in an untitled, incomplete manuscript in her Papers get called "episodes." In the back of booklet #2 of the *Nymphomaniac* series, along with other issues, Acker writes of them: "I want to and have been sending these books out for free dislike asking for money. I've now run out of money and people to borrow from. It costs approximately $100. to send out each of these *issues*. If you enjoy getting these and can spare the money, please do. *You'll receive* these of course whether or not you can help pay costs." Her emphasis. She signs this note, "The Fleshpots of Sin Return." In *The Burning Bombing of America*: "this working is a way of living." Elsewhere, in her Papers, she decides: "...I want writing to be a job like any other job. One is a worker." In the second part of the *Nymphomaniac* project, after detailing the difficulties of procuring a typewriter to do the work of writing, she claims: "I'm a poet and what I do is sacred. The people who keep me from the few lousy instruments I need to disseminate this crap are evil." Once more firmly established, for introduction of her students at a reading in the days before Tumblr and other people's platforms, other concerns, and filed now in the Serpent's Tail/ High Risk Archive, this was composed: "No government, no power historically has been able to stop printing presses, offset, and now desktop publishing. No one has been able to stop writing from erupting. This [sic] all writing occurs in the name of freedom. / And so the writers you are about to hear, in the name of freedom."

44.

In Memoriam to Identity: "And later all the business people would be after her obscenity judges bloodsuckers born-agains mealymouths her own dealers who had picked her up because she was famous but didn't really know what her work was would turn around and say, 'You're foul. You make our decency and decent society into something black. Stripper nymphomaniac. If you want, you can still join us the tea party of those who are known in even control this world, but if not, you are doomed." The "you" here, the artist Capitol, is a maker of doll, a metaphor that stands for the books over Acker's career, as we witness. *One of the smashed dolls was a Quixote, not the usual Quixote looking for love and purity in a society in which there weren't. In a society where language (the expression of ideals) and acts had no relation to each other. But a Quixote writhing, like one of Capitol's guts, into thinness from anger. A Quixote hating everything he knew,* not out of loneliness, *but in a world in which love and community had been so forgotten that the absence of love no longer occurred, was known.* Her emphasis, and here as well, where the artist, "could and would reply, 'I had training in puking and in saying *no* even before I was born.'"

45.

We might distinguish poems from songs, lyrics, which Acker's novels also include. Before the final account of "Don Quixote's Dream," the eponymous novel includes a score of dog and pirate singing. A poem by the character Ange *Pussy, King of the Pirates* includes, "'cause poetry is what *fucks up* this world." Shortly thereafter, Silver begins singing, the words lyrics on the page: *In their darkest hours, pirates rumbled love songs* it is told before being given one. Explaining her foray into music, punk singer Kathleen Hannah, once at the forefront of the Riot Grrl movement with the band Bikini Kill and later leader of the dance-groovier but still very unapologetically feminist outfit Le Tigre, in an article in *The Nation* gives Acker as catalyst due: "She asked me why writing was important to me, and I said 'Because I felt like I'd never been listened to and I had a lot to say... And she said, 'Then why are you doing spoken word— no one goes to spoken word shows! You should get in a band.'"

Reporter Hillary Frey, on the lyrics for Le Tigre's song "Eau d'Bedroom Dancing": "If the words sound like a poem you (ladies?) might have scribbled in your notebook at 14, consider these lines: 'No one to criticize me then / No one to criticize.' Sounds like a pop song, reads like a lament." Acker's *Florida* ends with the lyrics of a "stupid popular song...everyone was singing back where everyone was still living and burning each other out." Scholder's "Editor's Note" in *Essential Acker* begins with an inspired analogy of Acker's novels as concept albums, a link made more literal by Acker's collaboration with British punk band The Mekons, as whole sections of *Pussy, King of the Pirates* were set to music on an album of the same name. Artist and Mekon Jon Langford, who initiated this project with Acker, sums punk up in a discussion as "the willingness to do anything." When the album was reviewed, Acker's voice was praised as "a wonderfully flexible instrument" and the collaboration favorably compared to old children's recordings like *Peter and the Wolf*. The CD booklet folds out to reveal on the other side of the lyrics, *Ye Map*. Along with the drawings of fish and ships, pirates and mermaids, skeletons and hearts and dogs and crossbones, a written-out trace, you can get an impression of what went into making each song: samples used, arrangements, structures, mixing directions. Into the arena of the punk club, Acker brings such pleasurably shocking gems out there as the equation of squished roses and orgasm. In symbolic loops, feeding back in, embracing unabashedly before her listening audience desires, to take it further, a command—"off with their heads!" from the pirates or Red Queen—and a wash over Logos: *this is what an orgasm is. When the skin of inside the asshole comes out like a rose.* PUSSY: "Oh no, I shouldn't be doing this, coming out; asshole skin coming out; but it's okay

when it's an orgasm" ("Captured By Pirates," track #13). I feel
and hear Acker taking liberties even with the punks, exposing.
With the band behind her, she compacts the *Pussy* narrative,
unfolding it in different time signatures, with them trading off,
contrasting reference points, and varying risk. Pulled in comes
a sound bite, a British weatherwoman reporting imminent gale.
Who is ultimately steering is often hard to say, at the heart of
the ship, behind the mixing board. Given whispering, bedroom-
voice presentation of Acker dipping down to just above
moments of particular emphasis a growl, I transcribe as best I
can make out: *Inside is all field, cause there's constant* "journ,
yeah, in" *there*. Like all of the numbers narrated by Acker on
the record, in alternation with more structured songs from the
book performed by the musicians, "Captured by Pirates" does
not have printed lyrics accompanying the package. Checking
up against the novel, I find "journeying" I hear is *churning*, a
constant inside the field, or in the words of the number: "oh my
god bees." The contribution here of Acker highlights for me as
well the connotation often overlooked in coining of getting the
band together to play.

46.

In an essay draft in her Papers, Acker quotes Olson as saying,
"the private is public, and the public is where we behave." Or,
to a point: *Miss*-behave: *But, alive or dead, my pussy drips gold
and red and tastes like skunk.* These words are hers chosen to
print as part of a bookmark series that included Burroughs also
and poets Lyn Hejinian and Mei-Mei Berssenbrugge. In writing
on "Jeanne Duval," Acker makes it more explicit, in: "Play is
the opposite of ownership and that's why the bourgeois whose

sexuality is all about ownership hate us." She is on one of those reactive rants she takes for herself when, in *Memoriam to Identity*, the stand-in character decides: "Who gives a shit how your mother died or if you have a real father. Only stupid Oedipal-obsessive theorists care about that sort of thing." As much as her works try to assimilate it and move outside it, they desire and confront theoretical interpretation, in a movement not unlike the ambivalent relationship to mothering found in the books themselves. A complete picture, or holes in the story, holds evolve back-and-forth between passages of utterance, comprised of what she writes in novel patches and scripts of criticism along in interviews.

47.

We never are given just one, definitive version of the developmental narrative in Acker, but there are stories we come back to time and again. These repeats are her designs. The dance of a stripper makes up large parts of *Politics*, or at least the excerpt published in *Hannibal Lecter, My Father*. "Politics" is not part of the archive at Duke, not part of any other archive that I can find, and I have never seen it in an entirety. The strip finds its way as gainful employment into both *I Dreamt I Was a Nymphomaniac* and *Great Expectations*. *The Childlike Life of the Black Tarantula by the Black Tarantula*: "I leave my parents, then my husband, my career. I'm not very good at making money. I have two main problems: (1) how to earn $200 to $300 per month to eat, pay rent, without becoming a robot and with my clothes on...." Some things have changed in NYC. We are still then in the seventies. The stocktaking there is written in a section before the narrative moves itself to San Francisco, where prospects might be more *promising*: "All I talk about is money I'm moving to San Francisco I don't know how I'm going to live in San Francisco model I'll become a famous pornographer ha ha if I don't get the money myself I'll die starvation alone on the street I'm out of money right now." This parenthetical concludes that section of the story at present. In her essays, movement to San Francisco is "escape" and even a possible kind of utopia: *however weird a person thinks himself or herself that person will always find someone weirder in San Francisco*, in "Some American Cities," calling out a possible *provincialism*, yes, but that "lack of connection to corporate markets such as the New York art and publishing worlds, and a gay lifestyle are enabling San Francisco, for the moment, to combat the decay engendered by American postcapitalism and imperialism."

48.

Acker seems particularly confused concerning the earliest years, when she was just starting out and struggling to make a name. "I was the Black Tarantula before I was Rip-Off Red," she tells Lotringer. Conducted October 1989-May 1990, the exchange, titled "Devoured by Myths," serves as a preface of sorts for her Semiotext(e) publication, *Hannibal Lecter, My Father* (1991). The compilation includes an excerpt from what she there calls her first work, 1968's "Politics," beginning a mirror already between herself and those French seen as outsiders (who self-politicized along the informative lines of race, class, sexuality, how these are engendered), 1986's drama, "The Birth of the Poet," written for and directed by Richard Foreman (music by Acker's second husband composer Peter Gordon), translation of the German document (titled "Immoral") outlining a court decision in 1986 to place her 1978 copyrighted novel *Blood and Guts in High School* on its list of publications harmful to minors, and a number of other short pieces. This interview is an initial touchstone for me. The two of them are trying to date just how old Acker was, where she lived when she wrote what, who she was. "Oh memory, it gets everything mixed up." Seemingly just as confused as the constructions in some of her earlier fictions, "I don't remember, I honestly don't." The first thing she dates with certainty here: "Wait, I can remember exactly because that's when my mother suicided."

49.

In Memoriam to Identity, her Capitol, the female artist, and metaphor for Acker, lays out her motivations for reinterpreting what's come before her in the world she's been born into and asked, she feels, to take on all its preexisting terms. She sees herself expected to apologize "for hating ownership, for finding postcapitalist and Newtonian identity a fraud." Since it is a later work, and Acker, or "Capitol," has acquired a history of work behind her, to backtrack now, to take something back something was made out of before, means to in her mind also say she was sorry "for all her years of not only publicly hating an ignorant therefore unjust society but also of trying to make someone of herself." It is here that "I am an *other*" (Je est un autre) comes again, perennially relevant, in a parenthetical aside or realization, which Acker amends to accommodate the thought process displayed above. Yes, *she* is: at least twice removed. She is not Rimbaud, author of the phrase, and she is being told now she is somehow not an artist—of the ilk of the "old and rich" ones she is being humiliated for. IDENTITY: *but many artists don't make their own work.* Alienated from her assigned identity, Acker is now finding herself to be thrown out of an adopted one as well.

50.

In some of her interviews, Acker relies most on the designation *book* to describe her works, expectations less, only pages and words, how these two come together to interact with spaces around them. This is the case with McRobbie and with Lotringer after "novel" for *Rip-off Red.* Some of Acker's earlier works, generally discussed as novels, had not at the time of her interview with McRobbie been published in England at all, Acker would emphasize, stating how much of it was not then known. "Book" would also be the designation artist Nayland Blake uses for his shared project with her. "I had told her about a dream and she made a book out of it, a book that also embodied the dream I hadn't dared tell her about—the dream of belonging," as he explains in *Lust for Life.* Less surprising the generic confusion that exists in Acker's work becomes if we give her credit. One of the points it makes is of a problem with simple un-self-reflexive classifications.

51.

Acker's "New York City in 1979" displays a number of settings, a number of historical contexts, characters, and characteristics of divergent genres—play, manifesto, story, novel—her work, you see, as part of some strategy to make it, keep it NEW to us and herself expands and changes identity as it is formulating itself. There was the Pushcart Prize in 1981, though public literary awards after this would be few and far between. One further distinction listed on the 1996 version of her CV, supplemented in parts by her agent, is for 1975-1976 a "Creative Artists' Public Services Program New York State Grant For Fiction." In the work "Humility," ideas of which are incorporated into the ending movement of *In Memoriam to Identity*, that narrator begins to encapsulate in writing the ups-and-downs of the idea of career: *As a child in sixth grade in a North American school, won first prize in a poetry contest.*

52.

Acker calls *New York City* a short story in her essay "A Few Notes on Two of My Books." Elsewhere, others call it a novel. There is not much difference in length, though perhaps in scope, between it and *Florida*, whose great brevity does not prevent it being classified when collected eventually in the volume *Literal Madness* as one of *three novels*. It may be the shortest novel ever written. *Florida*: one character retreats, checks into a hotel, has a memory, prepares to settle into oblivion, decides love (a gangster) is life and escape, waits it out during a hold-up at the hotel—all in around 12-14 pages depending on book dimensions, the relative stage, if you like. What may prove to be the somewhat arbitrary rules of genre are those that Acker goes through in developing her body of work. If *Florida* is to be considered a novel, why not "Lust"? "Lust" gives us a drifter in *a sailor's slight identity* and displays even more settings— Germany, the church called "St. Marks-in-the-Bowery" (or the Poetry Project, as some will know it), London—before the poets and homeless, sailors and boxers and cops and revolutionary radicals and non-revolutionary radicals give way to another story inside, "Some Sort of Trial," which two children play at, followed by "Alterations of Reality and Childhood," where the boxer returns to the sailor and brings that *I* back to life. "Algeria," collected also in the *Hannibal Lecter* volume, is subtitled "a series of invocations." It moves far and wide between New York and identifications of, through, with the Algerian revolution before ripping bits from what we have come to know of Acker's biography. This is before scenes that take place in Algeria and New York and the Underworld in a version of *Black Orpheus* that invokes Levi-Strauss. A terrorist "CUNT" character plants a bomb in a cosmetic case in a bar. Acker employs in the piece "Algeria" both a first-person and third-person voice and connects characters through the designation *CUNT*: "THE CUNT my mother," "THE CUNT my grandmother," "THE CUNT companion," "a young CUNT," "CUNT Waitress," "CUNTS," "young boy-CUNT," and two peripheral characters also only identified by, but no further than: *CUNT*. The word also serves as a subtitle of sorts for the piece, before it really gets going: *Algeria / A series of invocations / because nothing else works // The land in Algeria is Pink / Life in this America stinks // Cunt // In, 1979 before the Algerian Revolution begins, the city is cold and dank....* Ellipsis in the original, all-caps in the above. The character with which Acker can be identified most clearly here is "Omar," whose mother suicides, whose wealthy grandmother "likes me when I'm married," i.e. still offers financial support, so Omar has to keep pretending to be married to *Ali*. The penultimate move will be to 42nd street's FUN CITY. When Acker performs the piece at Naropa University (6/13/1979), she cuts from Omar and Ali and the grandmother and her companion to the strip scene, the transition in the reading made by her saying something along the lines of, *So what are you gonna do? You got to pay the rent, right?* In fact, one of the written scenes she moves over, when comparing the structure of the published work, is Omar being confronted by "French Landlord." The archived sound file becomes identified as "selections," including a *poem*, "Sex Show."

53.

At the very least, there seems to be a marked distinction in Acker's mind between her books *Rip-off Red, Girl Detective* and *Politics*, in terms of genre. To Lotringer she claims *Rip-off Red* as the first novel she wrote, and we might take this as an interesting case of how the novel first comes into play for her, along what lines, what elements in her thinking must be in place seemingly and called upon. Being closer to more traditional contours is arguably the embarrassment of this novel ("Very luckily it has never been published"), though its form is not nearly as methodical as *Kathy Goes to Haiti* (1978), with a regulated back-and-forth of alternating chapters of two clear narrative forms and Acker's take on them, a travel book and a porn book. *Kathy Goes to Haiti* is one of at least two of Acker's "pornographic mysteries." *Rip-off Red* also qualifies here, as might the unpublished "Peter Gordon: Ambiguity," copyrighted 1984. *The agent for our business there, a Mr. Gluck, picked me up at the airport. Later that evening he took me to a night club. All night clubs in Istanbul were also brothels.* All sentences or paragraphs might also have trapdoors. How to determine the connection of this included parenthetical in following sentences? *(Bohr, the dada physicist, felt there was no real contradiction between science and art, said that as continuity is to discontinuity, logic is to instinct.)* And then: *Before I know what I'm doing, I have pulled out Mathis' revolver and fired it full in Banat's face.* In the Serpent's Tail/High Risk Archive, to correspondent "Bob": *You can look for* clues *to my feelings all you want, but you'd do better just to look at the facts.* Original emphasis. In *Kathy Goes to Haiti*, Acker tells McRobbie, she just wanted to write a Nancy Drew porn book. She also shows herself to disfavor the work, variously, but a letter to another correspondent, Paul Buck, informs, "I kind of have a policy to disregard what people say about my books cause it's always so coocoo, but I'm getting a little bugged at to what extent people don't see that KATHY GOES TO HAITI is a take-off on Nancy Drew plus stable porn: a genre piece, and therefore not simple, not really a novel at all: meant to be extreme of what the '20th century' novel is: psychology etc. so of course there's narrative etc." And, "KATHY GOES TO HAITI really is a nasty little machine and I shouldn't complain when machines react to machines...."

54.

She does not become a novelist overnight. In *The Burning Bombing of America*, "this is a doctrine call it what shit you want." In her introduction to *Young Lust* (a UK publication similar to America's *Literal Madness*, an opening aside and substituting though her *Toulouse Lautrec* piece in the place of her *Pasolini* work), she quotes a lesson ("among many") "learned by the time I was in my early twenties," "a practical one." She goes on to address money. Poets do not make it, she says. She backs up her conviction with a sharp paraphrase that colludes Rimbaud and Patti Smith in versed recognition in being that—seen as—that most offensive of off-color words. She also traces some connection to Fluxus. In her Papers, an untitled and incomplete manuscript asserts how by the age of twenty she knew she didn't want to be a poet, "for poets only talked to other poets."

55.

In her interview with Lotringer, Acker attempts to give some sense of another early work. "I was writing a book called POLITICS, which was little prose poems." And: "The center of POLITICS is a long autobiographical section about my life in the strip-show in which I was working." It is from the center section that the fragment produced in *Hannibal Lecter, My Father* later republished in *Eurydice in the Underworld*—a reprint of *Hannibal Lecter* minus the Lotringer interview, and additionally bookended by her "Eurydice" piece and "Requiem"—and the same fragment also excerpted in the reader *Essential Acker* seems most likely to have come. Situated in *Hannibal Lecter*, it is parenthetically classified: *MY FIRST WORK, WRITTEN WHEN 21 YEARS OLD.* It will not be a case of simple math. Not here or elsewhere (the letters to Paul Buck published as *Spread Wide*: "I am getting middle-aged I'm going to be 34!, I thought 33 and then Peter...came in town, and said NO, HONEY, 34, not 33"). Just backtrack twenty or twenty-one years to find out when she was born? The copyright for this *Politics* is 1968, marked unpublished, although it is listed elsewhere as having possible publication with a Papyrus Press in 1972. It is not part of the Duke archive. Research channels lead me to the University of Houston, where inquiries yield only a claim of there being no papers related to Kathy Acker there. "Recently discovered and never before published," Grove Press packaging says of *Rip-off Red*, though there is a "private" 1973 publication that has been documented. Acker does prepare and bind work before *The Childlike Life of the Black Tarantula*, copyrighting it at least for herself, if no one else, still work not yet seen to merit any larger-scale production. She types a "C" in a circle and a date and her name. Many of these earlier, preserved writings carry the subtitle designation of "exercises": *Writing Asystematically*, and *MURDERS RUN (ON) THE MOON: Exercise #6: Transformation of Sentences*. "Create music through repetitions of own sounds," she tells herself in another of the experiments preserved in her Papers. Here we may consider this to be her serving out something like an apprenticeship still under Burroughs and Gysin's *The Third Mind*. She will bring it up in interviews, how she did all of the prompts in the book. This was how she taught herself to write, she said before.

56.

In the concrete play of another early and unpublished piece in her Papers, by all appearances poetry and dated by Acker, from the Fall of 1972, "Entrance Into / Dwelling In / Paradise":

> *der*
> *I murmur*

she writes. An ultimate expression of impotent rage: murder, murder as a polar opposite of passivity, of being silenced, quieted. Acker sets this out in language, highlighting a matter of degrees found in syllables, how the constituents of language turn along a spectrum. In "Politics": *Mark comes up says that he thinks that no one if he didn't feel restrained would be normal.* She tells Lotringer, "No, I never wrote poetry, I always wanted to write prose."

57.

Like *Kathy Goes to Haiti*, the *Red* work is more an experiment with (rather than against, outside of, among) genres. The genre is the (girl) mystery-detective story. For all of its subversions— and there are some—there are further, formal transgressions *Rip-off Red, Girl Detective* does not yet commit. Acker's movement of deconstruction here settles into a playing field behind a sole pair of eyes mediating dream or reality, and its perception, which the reader may easily make out and track, regulated through one central character, one "I": Red, within the book. Such a commercial point, indispensable some might say in discerning almighty story, the one and only, Acker recuperates later in *Blood and Guts in High School* (1978). Speaking of plot with Larry McCaffery in *Some Other Frequency*, she says it "came about only in the final draft, where I put something like plot on top of everything. So I tried to make Janey seem like one person...." But dream, reality, sexual confusion, childhood and ecstasies sit somewhat more understandably astride one another in *Red*, keeping in the vein of a more realist tradition. Here the *I* does not die. In her Papers, "When my form changes, I die, I am we and no more separation is possible." The "I" does not change its form all that much, even if it does declare: *I'm going to change my name.* Then, "On the 18ᵗʰ of August I become a murderer. I've taken too much shit in this empire city." RED: "I become, shitheads, the greatest murderess (and detective) in the world."

58.

Putting aside these restraints in structural levels, as far as embarrassments go, there are also some passages in *Rip-off Red* that appear as supplemental to the EVIDENCE section repeated, with some variation, as part of *The Childlike Life of the Black Tarantula*. The piece marked "Age 11" is remarked "Age 12," some paragraphs of it cut, along with a sentence of describing a mother: *She turns to my sister: asks my sister to play cards with her and fetch her glasses of water.* The sister in both versions is made a "close friend" and "servant," but *beloved* in *Red* is "lover" in the *Black Tarantula* version. The repeated slur of "Whore," all capitalized or not, a period before a coming sentence or not, Acker shuffles childhood around. Beyond the somewhat reflective passages, *Red* has descriptions for "Ages 1 through 10," "Age 11," and two for "Age 16," as both chapters eleven and twelve are titled. Some data not repeated later in *The Childlike Life* found in going through the earlier *Red* involves the mother who "always wanted to stop being Jewish." "Clear," we are told, is the mother's name. During the narrator's year sixteen comes the disclosure about her parents: *My grandmother has bought them a summerhouse in Connecticut, a farm with real chickens and strawberries; they belong to an exclusive beach club, except that it's Jewish.* The narrator calls mother and grandmother *a cute couple.* It is not the mother but the grandmother who is the repository of art. It is she who lives by the *Mom-a.* She is "queen dyke of the family," and Acker's narrator gains an early vocational instruction through this grandmother figure, who "writes dirty poems," and whose books "teach me most of what I know at this early age." The grandmother character complicates the nuclear parental unit, as Acker gives in symbolization through the grandmother's "triple-person bed." In Acker's *Great Expectations*, "my mother wanted to remain her mother's child rather than be my mother." Just as Acker in her *Tarantula* phase would imitate "madness," the grandmother to get away with more is said to have "imitated senility." The *Red* narrator dreams of ways to have her mother stop *putting me down for my shyness and ways I act*. Red wonders in chapter nine "when I'll be old enough to get rid of my parents."

59.

In a section of "evidence" in *Rip-off Red* not repeated in *The Childlike Life*, the child's polymorphous perversity is given a full reign. In *Rip-off Red*, we simply can't tell if it's just a dream of Mommy or not. Left unclear is whether the fantasizing that begins with the narrator starting to "dream I'm Rip-off Red" continues or is interrupted by her mother's flesh entrance. The fantasy begins after nose-picking, rubbing it on her lips, feeling her as yet undeveloped breasts, playing with her belly-button and between her legs, and comparing the taste to cookies. Cookies and sex a conjoining that recurs over Acker's work. Like Acker is recorded as having for a short stint, Janey works in a bakery to comic effect in *Blood and Guts in High School*. IDENTITY: "When I was a kid...just before I was about to go to sleep, I would put the middle finger of my right hand, cause I was right-handed, into the wet softness between my legs, then lick my finger. The liquid tasted like the vanilla between the two chocolate sides of a Hydrox biscuit." The narrator character there is "Airplane," her father "the judge" she tells afterwards "I wanted to eat only Hydrox cookies." *My Death My Life by Pier Paolo Pasolini* (1984): "Why do Hydrox cookies taste like cunt juice?" That is in "The denial of sexuality" section. What's in a brand? "Mmm tastes like chocolate cookies, the Nabisco white-filled ones," in *Red*, followed in the next sentence with, "I don't like cookies."

60.

Messages with the mother also get mixed. Whereas in future books, a father or stepfather is progenitor of molestation and incest, in *Rip-off Red* we will go more rounds with Mommy. (In both *The Childlike Life of the Black Tarantula by the Black Tarantula* and *Rip-off Red, Girl Detective*, Acker writes: "My mother and I look almost exactly alike; we have many of the same characteristics.") Acker's intent, from the very beginning in her first identity experiments and tests, was to try to go around, outside or past "normal" plots provided for her. Enter Mommy, the dream and/or the bedroom, in *Red*. Mommy wants to know if her darling does anything else with the boy her darling has told her she kissed. *Mommy, did you ever kiss men; take their clothes off?* Her answer, "I wouldn't do that to my little girl." With the mother here is compared to "being wrapped in a blanket of white velvet skin," "an animal being taken care of by its mother animal." The childlike mind wants it safe to be this way, though the mother is also the cause of "the melting beginnings of my lungs until my breathing stops," molesting tongue compared to a "poison dart," invading the child's throat. *I don't want her to take off her clothes...I learn every inch of her mouth's warm insides, the damp softness of the sides, the strange roughness of her tongue...a maze in which I lose myself.* My ellipses. *I'm beginning to disintegrate,* Acker writes, as *Red* gets more and more wrapped up in its own rhythms: "I try to imagine my mother," "my whole shudders," "I become nothing I become whatever happens to pass through me." Similarly, when reading Acker at times, I feel. Towards the end of this scene, age, chapter, "I love my mother." RED: *we separate our bodies and she leaves.*

61.

One way that Acker's "Tarantula" work might be distinguished from her earlier, more *poetic* compositions like *The Burning Bombing of America* is that those before *The Childlike Life of the Black Tarantula* do not concentrate around issues of indoctrination into society (read: patriarchy) of a girl, child through traditional family units. The child-drag character, or *becoming-daughter*, and how it can relate to the dynamics of prostitution that Acker takes on is not yet the focal point. Introduced in *The Childlike Life of the Black Tarantula*, much of Acker's subsequent novel work also grounds itself out of this basing premise.

62.

The ongoing body is a maze which Acker has not yet reclaimed through her own embellishing, adoption of an eventual metaphor, the "labyrinth," a layered conceptualization of both the body's consciousness as configured through associations and the text's keep and store of such traceable sites. RED:

"My tongue disappears I'm sucking without breathing; all that matters is the sucking." RED: "something between in and outside me." To be impassive is imprisoning. "My mother wants to be a wall," Acker has one of two seven-year old girls write in "The Meaning of the Eighties," an essay comprised of letters between two fictional characters, Zoozoo and Linda. Another sample: "Today my mother met William Burroughs. She got, she said, invited to this dinner party which was all men. As the token woman." "She said William Burroughs has the intelligence of the sharpest knife she's ever met." The tough, stone fortification, that which surrounds—the prisoner might also try some nights to snuggle up next to that impenetrability, tender. You hit up against the walls, too. My mother is also now AWOL. Hear that poetry, even when you can't see it, singing to you. Acker instructs—herself—early on in *The Burning Bombing* to "follow desire wherever it leads you." As she notes on Jean Genet, whom she gravitates towards, queer exemplar of greatly finding a way to hold yourself inside a world of your own select kind, in her papers writing on his *Prisoner of Love*, "as usual he is speaking both directly and poetically." The breach in the walls leads to the desired bastard.

63.

A crime it might be to some in inscription to transgress outside symbolic imperatives. One "I" tells us in *The Childlike Life*, after an historical account of a murder: "I feel like I've done what I wanted. I feel elated. I've succeeded forgetting my parents." A proper woman does not do those things she desires to do, so flagrantly, as another code of conduct is adopted. She fashions herself as homosexual sailor in "Lust": *we're making signs to each other that we're unlike by displaying disease or murdering*. And: *By murdering I raise myself out of the death in which I'm living*. In her contribution to "Proposition One" (in *The Artist in Society: Rights, Roles, and Responsibilities*) she writes, "Both Baudelaire and Rimbaud posited themselves as writers against a society of power. They saw themselves, writers, as dandies, friends of whores, slackers—as anything but powerful." In *Pussy, King of the Pirates*, it is Artaud recognizing that Nerval desired to refuse his "cockhead."

64.

With a father as a be-all and end-all, options will be of necessity limited. In *Blood and Guts in High School*, "Never having known a mother, her mother had died when Janey was a year old, Janey depended on her father for everything and regarded her father as boyfriend, brother, sister, money, amusement, and father." In "Lust," in the opening subtitled "A Sailor's Slight Identity," we are told, "Because he's alone, a sailor's always telling himself who he is," before moving into first-person voice for the relating apparently of this state: *Due to the increasing conservatism of this government, the cops're enforcing more and tighter restrictions on every area of the private sector.* Here will be recounted for us *the life of vermin*. Capitol, in the "Girls Who Like to Fuck" section of *In Memoriam to Identity*, begins introducing her story: "Daddy was a drunk, and mom had decided to be a crip, but I didn't mind them too much. Quentin came back from Harvard with all these ridiculous *theories*. He told me Freud had said that all women are naturally masochists, though he didn't say that that simply."

With a short passage that explains, before part one ("Into That Belly of Hell Whose Name Is The United States"), Acker begins *My Mother: Demonology*: "My mother began to love at the same moment in her life that she began to search for who she was." R's mom, in "The Beginning of The Life of Rimbaud" (the opening section of *In Memoriam to Identity*), introduces his character by what she thinks of him, with lamenting, "a human homosexual," "the product of this dick," meaning the abandoning husband.

65.

Empire of the Senseless (1988), Abhor: "When daddy wasn't with me, he lived in a brothel. A sex-show was the brothel's front. Since the sex show actors had only fake sex, this sex show's legality was a cover for the rest of the filth which went on. / The desperate voyeurs who sought their sexual gratification in the masturbatory contemplation of a remote object...the degradation of the performers who not only put their flesh and minds on parade in the tradition of the Miss America beauty pageant but also were forced to watch this deterioration, this deterioration of themselves...." I cut in here. Here Acker is clear, through her character Abhor. The story is made even more remote by having the reader understand the connected Thivai is the one who is coming out with it, minding or mining it. Thivai tells us what Abhor said to him. Acker takes the show of the public strip, miming acting ready, as the veritable wellspring for the performers'— hired hands—internalizing of this alienation from terms of their own desires. Heightened, stewed, it is done in service of a frisson of transgression, a heady cocktail of shame or guilt or even the blasé disregard. You name it. It is revealed as the inside of the surface signs. Or at least that's how Thivai would have us to hear, to receive, his Abhor, her and her partners under control of an employ, for the time being, and he doesn't have to stay there.

66.

When I put down a word that cuts against the ingrained, or that goes both ways, the compass of bearings turns. You need to stop and stay, relax a while, look around rather than getting on to that next explicit, "real," action. "My father is not my *real father*," she emphasizes in *Some Other Frequency*. Her restlessness and desires will keep her going over her own dreams and memories, for her own self, in acts of definitional reclamation, putting them to her own uses, as she wouldn't want to just turn them over to the likes of some shod in Freud, who might, one fear, want us more awake all the better to produce the same old families more efficiently. If all a woman is vested for, according to the Law, is to have a baby, she must be something else. They must all be proved wrong. The father as more symbolic than biological would be no great help. She takes a page from a madman's lesson, in terms of what she can offer, in the Artist in Society conference speech: *Artaud has shown us that the political structure of this society is inextricably tied to the structure of that which first socializes, the structure of the family*. Her lack here, as lorded over her not only by narratives in psychoanalysis but also society's related images of the two-parent family as desirable and natural above all others underpins a conservative culture she sites. She goes further on in her speech, quoting from Artaud, "this world of mother-father is justly that which must go away, / for this is the world of split-in-two / in a state of constant disunion / also willing constant unification...."

67.

For his Rrose Sélavy, Duchamp asked around in borrowing from others, clothes, hat, ring, to appear in drag as the phenomenon conceded a collaborative effort. The creation of her does not belong to him, she is everyone's, remarked Mary Ann Caws at CUNY Graduate Center, September 18, 2006, in "an interdisciplinary afterword" to MoMA's Dada exhibit. As *I* artist, Acker borrows from him and his legacy. She places a quote readily associable with him, "I kept working on the 'Large Glass' for eight years, but despite that, I didn't want it to be the expression of an inner life," next to another utterance, one more apparently, the more you know, linked to Acker's own autobiography: "I keep trying to kill myself to be like my mother who killed herself." These moves Acker makes in her *Pasolini* work. Acker metaphorically fulfills the individual goals by having both statements issuing from a single shared character, a "speaker" marked for all indications one and the same, identified only, solely as "I." This cunning, formal balance of concerns appears just a couple of pages after Acker specifically evokes Duchamp, assigning to him a type of "autism," after the question is brought forth: *What is language?* In an essay draft in her Papers, Acker writes one answer: "Language is or involves a community of memory." Her language subsists within and simultaneously constructs her corpus, as she enriches the words and concepts. Of course I make a metaphor: arms and limbs of her prose, for greater, self, mobility. Acker writes, discussing her trilogy in the essay draft I have pulled from here: "By the third book, *Toulouse*, I rested where I was, in this sexual relation, so to speak, between chaos and the meaning that language is, this sexual relation we call identity." Words become insistent looking glasses that retain imprints, however subtle, however streaked, standing before them, and however discernable only in certain lights. Words are ready-mades to be re-curated and re-fused. Some words become little areas of pain, intensified or attenuated by the mosaics within which they are then dropped. Also in her Papers, describing her development over the projects collected as *Portrait of an Eye*: "I realized that I had been working almost irrespective of language, as if language was a clear mirror, an almost Augustinian notion. However, I knew language is not a clear mirror, not even a mirror except, perhaps, for the mirrors in Cocteau's films." Mirrors such as these are ones that you can go through, if you find yourself so persuaded, to follow after a death. Or they become ones we can dream up alongside, to awake into other places, outside enclosures we were once in before, ones that specters come forward from, or ones bodies can disappear before. The mirrors of language function as doors to other realms, reflecting both ways, before and behind them, something to smash for entry and escape. In Cocteau's vision, they become fields of water to submerge one's self in, glide and spring through. As one enters there the supposedly solid, the mirror, it does not shatter but ripples out then around you, and releasing a sound frequency that can surround and accounting for your energy in the entrance. These mirrors of Cocteau's with their permissive qualities are featured in a movie-version world as well, where a poet could live as fêted celebrity, mobbed for autographs, known by any and everyone on the street, "a national hero" to use the words of the Police Chief when Orpheus must stand before him as he has been accused of stealing words from a missing man's poem. Figurative blood is on those hands. In an underground interrogation, the court of Hades he lands eventually in, what do you mean by "poet," he is asked. Orpheus is to reply? It is almost the same thing as to be a *writer*: "To write without being a writer," Orpheus clarifies. In death, though, he will see how there is no almost. The underworld is where love is accounted for, for once and for all, as "OR," as Acker is to fashion him in one of her last compositions, sees. Only if one swears never to speak again of what one saw there will one be free from the fate of being kept down there, never re-emerging, as one goes from judge to instructing judge.

68.

In "New York City in 1979," Janey is an Everygirl of sorts of the time and place. Janey wants Johnny. The piece is evolving at one point out of a subtitle later dropped: "To Jeanne's Insulted Beauty." Jeanne (or *Jeane*, as it goes in some of the parts of the drafts) is arguably insulted further in the final, published version. Now when Baudelaire takes the stage of the finished product, she's left unnamed, placed among a cluster of demand-makers, "his parents, society, his mistress, etc." JD says in one of Acker's drafts: *I think, the loneliness is beginning to drive me crazy. Then I thought that all the great mystics and saints in order to learn wisdom went into the desert and went crazy and passed to the other side of craziness. / I got a job in this theatre that was part sex show.*

69.

To refuse to marry well is to decide, of some necessity, that you would try to make your own way. Acker writes in one of her notebooks for composing around the personage of Jeanne Duval: *Now I had to make money because money makes everything happen in this city & I had no idea how to make money.* Duval, famously that mistress Baudelaire gave syphilis to and then watched die, and romanticizing this all the while: I find the Duval drafting seminal, a place where Acker is first clearly beginning to pace out how to stretch her own, individual bits of concerns into greater forms of novels or books rather than "pieces, poems," if you will. She becomes one of Acker's Janeys by the time a version of her telling of this story is actually published. The way this is worked into "New York City in 1979" is covered in Acker's essay, "A Few Notes on Two of My Books." A sentence in the back of one of the Duval notebooks cues: *What is really going on in NY?* There are two notebooks for "Duval," one gray that wraps around in light pink strings. The other is not yet the 80-sheet, 8 ½ x 7 inches, 20lb green paper University Ruled Notebooks which Acker eventually moved to and within which most of the composing of individual segments of *Pussy, King of the Pirates* and later work takes place. They leave such an impression on me as a particular moment of recognition, being of the same kind I first began keeping my own daily journal in back in undergraduate days. In her "Shit On My Sleepmask" essay, Kraus notes of a writing container that she knows of as once having belonged to Artaud, "Because it is so ordinary, the notebook has a magical charge. It is one of those kid's notebooks with multiplication tables on the back cover." She also gives a thumbnail of one of Acker's: *National Brand, spiral, narrow-ruled.*

70.

Authorship, across the covers of Acker's books, moves along lines of unstable signatories. *The Childlike Life of The Black Tarantula* by The Black Tarantula becomes, eventually, through business channels, *The Childlike Life of the Black Tarantula by The Black Tarantula* by Kathy Acker. *The Adult Life of Toulouse Lautrec* by "Henri Toulouse Lautrec" (Kathy Acker) undergoes a similarly signed, nested, metamorphosis. The point of origin, with which truth ultimately lies, might always be called into further and for further questions. "Do you know that *Books in Print* lists your books twice?" Acker is asked when interviewed in *The Review of Contemporary Fiction* (Fall 1989). "It lists *Black Tarantula* by an author called Black Tarantula and then has a listing for *Black Tarantula* by Kathy Acker. The same with *Toulouse*," Ellen Friedman tells her. This special issue is devoted to the work of Acker, Christine Brooke-Rose, and Marguerite Young. She writes and publishes herself early on in her career under a host of constructed personalities, the "Rip-off Red" of that novel attempt, used also in early notebooks and letters, hyphen sometimes, sometimes not, the imprint many ways in manuscripts, letters, and miscellanea. "Rip Red East" she jots down in one early notebook. Stationary for correspondence is headed with a return address of "Red's Detective Agency, Inc." Later in her career, as seen in correspondence held in the High Risk/Serpent's Tail Archive, she sent work off to her agent: *Hot off the fried mind press named Acker.*

71.

Still working under the cover of her more overt, signed authorial personas, the third section of the *I Dreamt I Was a*

Nymphomaniac project had both as its title and author "Peter Gordon," husband at the time, though the copyright it is given rests with The Black Tarantula. Acker later amends to a copy of this particular section in the archive at Duke, "Not by Peter but I said by him as a present to him. I was always changing my name in those days." *Rip-off Red, Girl Detective* when published by Grove Press is without a dedication found on the title page of the manuscript, at least as it is bound as her part of her Papers: "For my brother, Peter Peter." A dedication in another one of the *Nymphomaniac* standalone booklets reads, "This is for CP & PP who has to be around 1 day a week: this will make him be around." The fourth one is acknowledged as, "for the person who helped me do this." Authorship, as it never is, did not begin either as a sole endeavor for Acker it seems, but some tracks are lost in the pictures that remain of broader circulation, with only two dedications opening books existing in mass circulation, for *My Mother: Demonology* ("to Uma") and *Empire of the Senseless* ("to my tattooist").

72.

In a feature in *Publishers Weekly*, noted is how Acker had a jeweled tongue literally (amethyst on the setting of the day). One interaction with a prominent mainstay of more mainstream publishing, told here is how the Russian formalist Roman Jakobson once graded her papers. Prominence of periodical does not necessarily equal factual felicity. One glaring mistake or telling slip: *Lecher* is the word given as in her Semiotext(e) title. Her second husband is called "Peter Cooper." The report mentions too how Acker had sold cookies for a while, as one source of employment. See the "Mindless

Salesgirl," who works in the bakery in the *Blood and Guts in High School* book. In Acker's apartment, the writer spies a gray stuffed shark. That rhymes with a line in a postcard Acker sent to poet David Trinidad: *I just bought a stuffed rat, otherwise everything the same.* That reminds me of a passage in *Pussy, King of the Pirates*: "No, what she adored was to lay for hours in water. When, where there were lots of odors, those of the night, of owls hiding their eyes behind their own feathers, of rose lavender rosemary, of the buds that bloom in the dark. Of the evening and of dreams, snakes in search of rats who were no longer stuffed, leaves drenched in the liquid mud that was falling out of the sky." SENSELESS: "Dinosaur, who was a stuffed animal, was sitting next to us. Dinosaur was female therefore a prostitute." In this novel, a sex scene evolves then on the bed, one in which Dinosaur naturally takes part, a scene made more complicated on the page in the belly-button, remnant of umbilical cord, being figured as an entrance to a sexual possibility, where, interestingly given the shark above seen: *Tiny white shells appeared in that monstrous sea. 'My little dead shark. Better than dead fish.' I whispered to her while I fucked her in her asshole.* Dodie Bellamy performs a reading of the scene in a piece called "Can't We Just Call It Sex?"—the title coming from a prompt Acker inscribed following another question she also asked in dedication, "New Narrative?"—signing Bellamy's copy of the book within which this scenario appears. The different animals enter dreams and writing ("interstitial intelligence," Carla Harryman calls the rat figure prominent in *Pussy, King*) because one might guess Acker kept those furry, soft, pliable representations of them asleep in the bed with her, there among the pillows. "Eurydice in the Underworld," italics in the original: *There, rolls onto her left side and encounters a wolf. Puts her arms around him, as she's accustomed to do because he's faithful to her and because she knows he won't leave her whatever she does or whatever has happened to her.*

73.

As concerns she worked with over her entire career: the mythic criminal, the classic demagogue, their uncanny simulations added to and supplemented by her understanding in processing of Black Mountain and L=A=N=G=U=A=G=E schools of poetry, Beats, and then the Art World and its attendant poetics Acker also grafts in. In an essay, "Blue Valentine," Acker tells how, "I dreamed about New York City because New York City was Andy Warhol..." And also uncovers: "Until I started writing this, I had never realized how much Andy Warhol's work and ethos shaped my own writing and life." In *Don Quixote*: "I was a member of a certain group—the art world—whose members, believing that they're simultaneously society's outcasts and its myths, blow up their individual psychologies into general truths." She wrote the occasional article for *Artforum* and this brings with it honor of gracing one of their *Real Life Rock: Top Ten* lists, column space largely dominated by Greil Marcus, though also contributed to by her friend R. U. Sirius who includes Acker's *Pussy, King of the Pirates* in the October 1995 issue on his list of eccentric cultural radar offerings, highlights and interests: a drug, "The Return of Michael Jackson," to give an indication of a few others in those days of the CD-ROM. This gathering publicity somewhat misrepresents in placement on the book's jacket copy with its being "chosen as one of *Artforum*'s top ten books of 1995." Elsewhere, in an untitled and incomplete manuscript in her Papers, attempting to situate her praxis, she paraphrases another's idea: "Art was a finger pointing to the moon. If any artist did anything else, for the sake of prettiness, commercialism, etc., he or she was unfaithful to his or her concept."

74.

Like the field, the land of the page, and all its attendant breaking-off, there is an expanse in the self to work, 'til, explore, to track, account for, try to mend, make new dreams within. "There it is, brothers, sitting there for USE," as Charles Olson writes in his "Projective Verse." There is Rimbaud, sitting there for mine, in the field of literature (art). His most famous phrase, giving what's been called his *Lettre du Voyant* its *raison d'être*, is an encapsulation by Rimbaud, floated as both announcement and tease. It turns out it was made a couple of times. Once it was to his teacher, Georges Izambard, May 13, 1871, and then again he repeated it to friend Paul Demeny, May 15, 1871. He wants to make sure someone gets it. "It's wrong to say *I think:* one should say *I am thought.*" Lacan, with Descartes, makes his own and very similar move like this. *I* is thought. *I* is someone else. Or, given another translator: *I* is an *other*. Rimbaud puns around with "penser" (to think) and "panser" (to groom). Then, excusing himself: *pardon du jeu de mots*— forgive the play of these word games.

75.

Other texts of Acker's were self-produced, awaiting no one else for publication. I could begin to try to track them all down.

Hardin lists one called "Roman Day: Security and Punishment" that I have never come across. In her papers at Duke: "most privately printed / in fact not even well typed," reads a note following the dating to copyright "The Seattle Book," "for Randy and Heather." This piece begins with a versioning of Acker's ESSAY ON WRITING / the invisible universe, before working its way into letters to Alfred de Musset and others. Rimbaud in his Lettre du Voyant took on Musset, decrying the "angelic sloth," "tedious tales," "proverbs," "his Nuits," "Rolla." "Every grocer's son can reel off something Rollaesque, every seminarian has five hundred rhymes hidden in his notebook. At fifteen, these passionate impulses give boys boners; at sixteen, they've already resolved to recite their lines with feelings; at eighteen, even seventeen, every schoolboy who can write a Rolla does—and they all do! Some may even die from it. Musset couldn't do anything: they were mere visions behind the gauze curtains: he closed his eyes." Emphasis in the original, I quote Wyatt Mason's translation, though note where Schmidt in his renders "hard-ons." In "The Seattle Book," Acker begins one of her own seer letters to Musset, "I adore your cock." "If you go away from me for more than ten hours, I'll die." She then adds a new love interest to Musset's relationship with George Sand by working in letters she imagines from Flaubert to her. "Dear George Sand, / Your cock is too large for me. It isn't true women can stretch to accommodate any cock size: I'm not a woman and I can't stretch to accommodate anything." We will go on from here, in this essayistic work, of which Acker's fantastic, crudely philosophical letters are only one part of what will be revealed, to arrive at an injunction to "Define to love." She underscores in her original. Acker begins to do this by exploiting, and upsetting, comfortable rhetorical models of logic. For example, after the opposition "love of knowledge" versus "love of sex" is established to mirror— Acker's word—the: *mind : body* opposition, Acker decides such a separation is resolved by the fact, as demonstrated by the logical progression of her next sentence, that: *The lovers of knowledge and the lovers of sex both love cats.* Other oppositions, and their resolutions through third terms, follow. Acker does what she says she will do here: "Define to love by increasing complexity." This accomplishment of increase she demonstrates exponentially on her page through the equations and their circling back on themselves to contain themselves and all other formulations that came before them. This is not unlike the proposition eventually exhibited in "Narrative Breakdown," a section of her *My Death My Life by Pier Paolo Pasolini*: "One. One and one. One and one. One and one. One and one. One and one. One and own. One and one. One and one. One and one. / One and one and one. One and one and one. One and one and one. One and one and one. One and one and one. One and one and / One and two. One and two and no more." And so forth. Peep here amidst the sentence the line break, in the second paragraph. A cadence of thought is marked. Stein comes to mind.

76.

I have not yet wrapped up here, with "The Seattle Book," as we move through logic on to psychology. After discussing, in a convincing reproduction of clinical language—or just as likely moving into an unattributed "rip-off"—how personal pronouns present for the child "important difficulties," Acker drops the reader down to look around in Pooh-land, proving to be both playful and illustrative—the childhood lesson loaded—with her appropriation of the yellow bear and his gang. This stretch is then intercut, interrupted, by a picture that announces EEYORE and directs he is looking for his tail in our illustration. Hear this lovable character also called "The Old Gray-Purple Donkey, Eye-Eeyore" (I, 'e, or...), and read of him "pissing." Acker uses her figures from childhood as well to re-dress the idea of aphasia, introduced earlier into the piece, now through a more parabolic conversation between Owl and Pooh. "Owl, wise though He was in many ways, able to read and write and spell his own name WOL [sic], yet somehow went to pieces over delicate words like MEASLES and BUTTERED TOAST." Then Pooh nods towards the conclusion, as we say a goodbye to Seattle. As did Acker, where she once lived not very happily with a man, as she details in *Spread Wide*. We exit the piece with an unidentified paragraph I find to be from "Act I, The Woodcutter's Cottage" of Maurice Maeterlinck's fairy play *The Blue Bird*. Along the way to her ending, Acker paraphrases and quotes others like Descartes and Keats.

77.

In *Blood and Guts in High School*, the meaning of an "Ode To A Grecian Urn" is taken up in an illustration. A drawing is given this title as its caption and its own page, for a naked woman, up above her head arms raised bound at the wrists, ankles and lower legs similarly roped. Can I or not think of the Keats, to that title turn: *on*, slight though a twist may be. Taking up the left-hand side of this spread of the book, a drawing opposite this one, is another illustration executed similarly, with the heading: *Girls Will Do Anything For Love*. Between dark chalking hints of legs of body on its back, a dotted pattern below for pubic patch, She more deeply impresses and front and center insets folds of labia. I will not go over the father's penis, also taboo to uncover, though Acker will draw one or two, three, of those as well in *Blood and Guts in High School*. "The obvious depictions do not leave anything to the reader's imagination," the illustrations like these ones I've set out here, the court document banning the book says, in a translation.

78.

By the time Acker's novel *Blood and Guts in High School* is completed in 1978, some of her early, documented poems have become part of the fabrication of this work. Signed now by Janey Smith, the book's fictional character in the main, "The Persian Poems" change status in their attribution here as they become housed within this prose. Granted the ability to write a suite of poems, the Janey character finds another realm of linguistic expression. Other verse migrations happen elsewhere. Acker's poem of "Ali and the Mosque" becomes one component cell in "Act Three" of Acker's play "The Birth of a Poet," incorporated along with another poem marked as a persona, "The Arab Woman's Song for Her Lover Who Is Away [Far] from Her." In *The Poets Encyclopedia*, she has work among the ranks of Charles Bernstein, with his entry for "Casablanca" which is akin to Acker's take on *Key Largo* (motion picture) in her short *Florida*. Not so surprising is Burroughs's examination of "Junk," though sweetly resonant there is Ginsberg on "Junk Mail," Creeley's "Stubble," and Charles Henri Ford's "Anal Intercourse." The cover of the volume advertises: *finally the world's basic knowledge transformed by 255 poets, artists, musicians, & novelists.* On "Frost": Barbara Guest, and "Porcelain," too. Carolee Schneemann's "Knitting" is a photograph captioned: *Two women knitting on a Trailways bus, one said: It will all make sense when it is finished...I think.* In 1975, Carolee Schneemann pulled out her infamous "Interior Scroll." Years earlier, Acker was already twinning apparently, writing in *The Burning Bombing of America,* designated variously in sections of its body as "diary," as well as "ABSTRACT ESSAY COLLAGED WITH DREAMS," dated inside itself by her ("a place of rest. end. 5/72," "6/17/72"): *out of her gorgeous hairy cunt comes a papyrus.* In "Theoretical Grrrl," in *The Village Voice,* November 6-12, 2002, C. Carr knows Acker and Schneemann met in the mid '70s. Acker loved Schneemann, Matias tells me, 5/18/15.

79.

First published as a chapbook in 1983, "Implosion," like "The Birth of the Poet" (1981, staged by Richard Foreman in 1985), has three acts. The "Implosion" acts are further divided into three scenes, ten scenes, and two. Stage directions appear and seem meant to function primarily like that. The play form is incorporated into the novelistic enterprises, and Acker puts such scenic divisions to good use in advancing both narrative time and drama. In *Blood and Guts in High School,* the chapter entitled "In Egypt, the end," after an initial establishment of this section's scenario, is broken down further into a number of wide-ranging moments marked as scenes, 1-10. "Implosion" itself, in almost its entirety, becomes scene 11 of "Violence," the third part of the "Nominalism" section of the "My Death" book in *My Death My Life by Pier Paolo Pasolini*—an effort unwieldy I would say even by Acker standards. Here too is *Hamlet*, partly transposed to "The art world of New York City," before the book then begins to work itself at a point into a kind of *Romeo & Juliet*, returned to later in progress in French, in which "Orlando," "Heathcliffe," and "Catherine" are now briefly characters, before eventually giving away to "I" and "Nurse" roles. Also appearing is a version of *The Merchant of Venice* under the heading of "Adult Now (For Arabia)" and a "Teenage Macbeth."

80.

In *Blood and Guts in High School*, dialogue is designated also like lines to be spoken in a play, the characters summoned, any emotional qualification kept to parenthetical italics. Beginnings of new scenes are often established in the manner of stage settings, as striving after more immediacy for the encounters to follow. *Inside a small East Village bakery*: customers like the "Fat Lady" (*What's in that cooky there?*), "Thirty-year-old Man" (*Every time I come to this bakery, nobody pays any attention to me*), "A Thin Young Woman" (*I want ten loaves of rice bread, a dozen bialies, three dozen assorted cookies, two vegetable juices, and two sandwiches wrapped to go. I need it now*), and the "Twenty-year-old Whore-like Jew Lady" (who wants to know consequently if our salesgirl behind the counter is a whore). They come in and out, making up the workday of "Lousy Mindless Salesgirl." We hear her among other things having to turn it on for "Middle-Aged Shrivelled Man": *Certainly, sir.* Acker makes the world of her novel a stage, as characters who people the bakery take places in walking boards, pulling out personalities, the omnipotent set-designing author stepping back from the action, this all seen in a grander scheme and giving her perspective of things from which to disdain "people" such as: "A Wispy Blonde Hippy Girl," or "Parisian Hippy Salesgirl."

81.

In her work with *Great Expectations*, a domestic drama Acker shows unfolding, *Back in New York City, the tenth floor of an apartment building on 73rd street and Third Avenue*, stands in great contrast to the exotic escape passages which were more leisurely unfolding before, palpably not scripted of: "EGYPT," the nightclub "the Palace." "Dazzling sun effects." "Being allowed to laze. This' what it's about." "I live like a plant filling myself with sun and light with colors and fresh air." It follows back there in the *horror that is New York*, the HUBBIE and WIFE knowing the lines: "But you can't leave me. It's Christmas." Scene 2, The Husband's Monologue: WIFE is still presented in a staging as speaking, interruption. This formal sense employed here is echoed somewhat in the late "Eurydice in the Underworld." In "Eurydice's monologue," a scene of a single confidence: *About five weeks ago, on March 30, a biopsy revealed that a mass less than five cm. in my left breast was cancerous...* Ellipsis in the original, and ORPHEUS interrupts, proceeding to dominate through the space of speech—holding forth lyrically for the rest of the duration of this scene not technically his.

82.

In *Great Expectations*, Acker cuts from a section designated as "Mr. Anwar Sadat's monologue" to another letter to Peter, moving from the isolation of one political interior to the statement: *I'm finding it very hard to live without you.* Some personages in this book are those that are reduced to a sum of their parts in gender ("SHE," "HE") or "PROPERTIUS," "AUGUSTUS," "MAECENAS" accompanied by chatty Roman whores. Following *Great Expectations*, in her *Don Quixote*, Acker puts the dramatic conventions to more pointed use. In the play-like field of the WEDEKIND'S WORDS part characters Lulu, Schön, The Maid, Schigold, Alwa, Witch-Bitch, Thin Bitch, and Young Girl are; elsewhere long stretches in the work where no name at all is given to the left of the colon that cues a start to mouthing. The line originates from some elsewhere. Just exactly where this other body is, to whom it belongs, it is understood is erased, left to the air. This formal technique thematically underscores the FOR THOSE WHO LIVE IN SILENCE part. Lines of speech hang on the page to the right side of the colon—speakers on the left-hand, or living side, occluded. Gone also are their names, the Prince in a subsection marked "*THE LEOPARD*: MEMORY" no longer privileged to completely make out the "material," reality (*What People Say About Me After I've Died*).

83.

She writes in *The Adult Life of Toulouse Lautrec by Henri Toulouse Lautrec* (1975): "Suddenly I noticed some man's eyes on me. / He looked straight. I decided he was a creep. / He said...I'm Ron Silliman.... / ...I got to know Rae Armantrout, one of Ron's closest friends, who's bi like me. We hung out together. I guess I got to know Ron gradually. My closest friend at that time, *Clay*...." And I have gotten now to a name I want to know more about. In "I Don't Believe You'll Do The Same," a booklet like the Tarantula self-publications, the author "Clay Fear" writes: *I call myself an artist of many sides.* Clay Fear also writes: *This is the discipline of an artist today.* Some list "Clay Fear" as one of Acker's earlier pseudonyms, though this seems to be a real-world individual, not one culled or called up from the imagination. The writing when looked at differs in tenor to me. I find it somehow more *conscious*, somehow more at ease with the psychological concept from which to proceed, succinct, and in places in vocabulary out of step with Acker's lexicon. Some comparative examples I pull. *Watching a vampire movie is no substitute for having sex*, from Fear to: *As soon as the movie started, I wanted to lay my head on Johnny's shoulder, but I was scared he didn't want to feel my flesh against his*, from *Blood and Guts in High School*. Johnny and the first-person narrator Janey in "New York City in 1979," this time not dad and daughter, but going to an all-night movie, *Some Like It Hot* followed by *The Misfits*: "All during the first movie Janey's sort of leaning against Johnny cause she's unsure he's attracted to her and she doesn't want to embarrass him (her) in case he ain't." From Fear: *President Kennedy and Jacqueline Kennedy serve as pepper and salt shakers*, as opposed to: *Good liberal parents: they don't read much, but they think Kennedy could have saved the world.* Acker, in wanting to make a symbolic order act out in unruly ways, so to speak, goes to upset the dinner table, when she starts naming names. When an *art objet* is made of the first lady, as she would be in a section of *The*

Adult Life of Toulouse Lautrec, the heading that introduces the transformation in staging to this next starring, how one O. feels zero, exclaims for her: I WANT TO BE RAPED EVERY NIGHT! President Carter has "a shriveled little thing, a dried apricot pit that Richard Nixon VOMITED up" and he *abandoned me*. Reagan is an "evil enchanter" in the land of her *Don Quixote*. Bush, Sr. is a father who *rapes* in *My Mother: Demonology*. I can only imagine but would have relished seeing what she could have done with the junior. Going through the reader of selected Acker writings, I find no glaring appearances of the fraught word Fear bandies in, "He goes to big egos to have his ego fed." And the feeling *places where I live...can be like wombs* is likewise perhaps too simply stated an elucidation to find function in Acker's writing. Her character relationship to being carried, held, the "womanly," and asserting individuality in a face of such metaphors of embodiment prove over her corpus much more alienating and potentially fraught as they are unfolding dimensions for exploring. For example: *The coral reefs stretching into the sea look like mirrors of my cunt, my inner womb; then look utterly strange: black sea monsters skimming the surfaces of each other's bodies for their communication.* And: "a knife toward my womb I feel nothing I arch my back so that the top of his cock presses against the upper part of my cunt, the delicate opening of the skin below the cunt hairs, I'm scared I move back and forth quickly abandon myself to his rhythm as his legs tense, my tensed muscles the muscles around my clit shooting outward disintegrate I lose my sex by coming" (these passages from *The Childlike Life*). You could compare Fear's, "The dog won't learn to take care of herself," to these two summations ushered in *My Mother*: "And if dreams are dead, for the moment, I'm going to climb upon Chance, whose dog I will always be." And: "I am now free to be mad and I will go to him and lay myself at his feet and say, 'I'm your dog.'"

84.

Acker's life story would seem to follow the form of her fictional output, or vice versa, as one was folded into the other, as she continued to explore, in increasingly complex ways, interconnections. One constitutes, determines, inflects the other. This system of circulations is further flexed and stressed as others, in her absence, take her into their own communities, and by that read their own books too, their own fiction and knowledge, truth claims. It is hard not to address Acker and Sylvère Lotringer when they come up again in Chris Kraus's 1997 hybrid-diary-manifesto-letter-novel *I Love Dick*. Ostensibly the *real* subject of Kraus: British media theorist best known for his book *Subculture: The Meaning of Style*, Dick Hebdige writes to my author as she is dying, "Take good care, Kathy. I wish you the very best of luck on whatever journey lies ahead." Correspondence, Papers. Browsing through a Lotringer character's books, first name sans accent there, a Kraus narrator "realized she was up against some pretty stiff competition, reading some of the inscriptions: 'To Sylvere, The Best Fuck In The World (At Least To My Knowledge) Love, Kathy Acker.'" Kraus is arguably who Acker is trying to get at when in *My Mother: Demonology* she writes: *My sense of the ridiculous, or loneliness, extended to personal relationships: one of my ex-boyfriends, another tour member had abandoned me for the woman who was now his wife and who was about to meet him in three days.*

85.

"We like to mention each others' names," the author known as Clay Fear writes in "I Don't Expect You'll Do the Same." In the back of the booklet, above the information on how to reach the creator, The Black Tarantula is given thanks. Inside the cover binding it is the beseeching: "Since I am here mention me." To return to my previous stage, Kraus proves to be not shy at all about dropping, indeed driving, Lotringer's name into her just as unclassifiable and ribald as Acker work: *I Love Dick*. Why should she be? As she states in an interview about her authorial methods, as they are rising to prominence, "The only thing I thought I could offer was a willingness to report on my subjective experience with some precision." The assertion is to a connection of his valuation of worth. If we might like to proceed so conservatively, and divisively, Kraus even performs what could appear to be her trump: "For months my husband Sylvère Lotringer has been carrying around one of Antonin Artaud's famous notebooks in his backpack." Diacritics reappear in essays like the one this from, "Shit On My Sleepmask." I stress this spousal assertion, though I believe also a closer connection to Artaud might be tied in here too.

86.

One of the dedicatees of Ron Silliman's edited volume *In the American Tree*, Hannah Weiner does an entry in *The Poet's Encyclopedia* for "Ampersand" consisting of the word presented handwritten, cursive. Appearing to not use only English, Acker also prides in the same venue the manual. She closes her take on the imprisoned, racked body, the enslaved mind subjected through the motions of one form bending another, and that extends to cultures, with a graphic sign. It could be to me just as much a picture as it could quite possibly be the mark of letters, one or more, some such constellation. The limits of my Western, trained, eye does not know exactly how to make of it. This finishing flourishing of Acker's is not reproduced in *Blood and Guts in High School*. Though a version of the piece does exist here, it does not come to the same conclusion shuffled in part into the body of the book. After the first thirteen paragraphs or lines, depending on orientation of your view, taking it up to the sentence "I might as well not exist," the work begins to undergo a mutation in sentence orders and omissions until cut off by the parenthetical closing-down of that one which began around an italicized designation cuing us to read what we are as what *Janey* writes while being held captive. Readers are returned to a previously interrupted "A throw of the dice never will abolish chance," one of the poems we are told in *Blood and Guts* Janey wrote by herself, Acker's riffing on Mallarmé's seminal "Un Coup de Dés."

87.

Before Acker's increasing stature as a literary presence would occasion further collection of the three of her early works together, the first series of pamphlets (*The Childlike Life*) and last work in *Portrait of an Eye* (*The Adult Life*) were each published as complete books by The Vanishing Rotating Triangle Press. Others published by them would be John Ashbery, Guy Debord, and even Charles Manson. Prior to *Portrait of an Eye* from Pantheon, *I Dreamt I Was a Nymphomaniac* is given a complete publication by Traveler's Digest Editions. Though later many of Acker's books contain her own artwork, drawings, handwriting, floor plans, maps, tattoo designs, figured signs, the 1978 publication of *The Adult Life of Toulouse Lautrec* (back cover: "all she wants is love...") included drawings by William Wegman: a drawing of a label headed "PLEASE HELP ME," with marked lines for Name, Address, City, State, Zip; a hybrid woodpecker-swan; a toddler holding a couple hostage and captioned as such; a heart that says inside of it, "I Love you." She draws her own hearts too. In Acker's projected "Book of Correspondences," which was to be in part a comic strip, bits of which are in her Papers, she draws a "Double heart that's piercing itself," as she clarifies in the legend of sorts she scripts in accompanying intention. In *Pussy, King of the Pirates,* crossbones become hearts, as again a lettered message accompanying the drawing points us further in those attentions we might bring towards the meaning of a sign. Back in the early edition of *The Adult Life of Toulouse Lautrec by Henri Toulouse Lautrec*, Wegman does a scripting of "Chinese Food" where the "C" and "F" are characters. Approximations, in another language I don't know? Now I am faced with that knowledge, or make the decision that is what it stands for, filling in the blanks, or leaving that open, an experience similar to reading the non-Western alphabet making up the signature given to and part of the piece that was published as "Slavery." The Persian alphabet features in *Blood and Guts in High School*, Arabic in *Empire of the Senseless*, Farsi lessons in *My Mother*. A branch flowers simultaneously, the viewing reader is instructed by her illustrator in Wegman into monkshood, mistletoe, myrtle, millet, mountain laurel, and marigold. Rimbaud's "Alchemy of the Word" is fruitful, to consider how Acker practices and writes what could be said to be alchemy of a Symbolic. Rimbaud: *I loved idiotic pictures, fan-lights, stage scenery, mountebanks' back-clothes, sign-boards, popular coloured prints, old-fashioned literature, Church Latin, ill-spelt erotic works, romances of the time of our grandfathers, fairy-tales, little books for children, old operas, silly refrains, ingenuous rhythms.* The poet minds: *I arrested moments of vertigo.*

88.

Another helpful link, beginning to see how to generously read Acker, what she was going for, hoped or guessed she might provoke, desired effects intended in what lights, what was afoot around her: Cindy Sherman, though links could be drawn and seen also studied later in life through Kahlo, whose biography Matias records her to have been reading in the hospital. Sherman and Acker are paired up pictorially when Acker's essay "Realism for the Cause of Future Revolution" is given first publication, in *Art After Modernism: Rethinking Representation.* Here it is accompanied not only with reproductions of the paintings Acker's essay explicitly discusses, Goya from his "Black" period, along with Caravaggio, but a reproduction, at its conclusion, of one of Sherman's photographs alongside a picture of its inspirational basis. Sherman is making herself look a boy. *Devouring Institutions: The Life Work of Kathy Acker,* Hardin's anthology was initially to feature "Untitled #216, 1989" of Sherman's *History Portraits* series, a blond Madonna with disconcertingly plastic-appearing breast exposed poised, centered, appropriation of a painting by Jean Fouquet (dated 1450, 1452) as cover, before replaced by the much-ripped-off screaming piece of Munch. Sherman intersects with Acker in two other forums of publicity. The periodical *FILE*, published 1972-1989 in Toronto, featured excerpts of Acker's work and in 1982 a six-page Sherman portfolio. Sherman's *Sex Pictures* of 1992 would be the source providing a German cover—one of a male head locked down atop round doll breasts and genitals "lifelike"—for Acker's *My Mother: Demonology*. Acker writes in her 1990 essay, "Critical Languages," "Returning to New York City in January, hungry for New York's art community, or rather for my memory's vision of New York's art community, I ran from gallery to gallery. Sherri Levine, Richard Prince, Jenny Holzer, etc. Artists from whom I had learned much. I now saw that these works equaled money." We might think of the Acker books too in terms of diorama, the time capsule, scrapbook impressions saved. *I love my camera—it is like a paintbrush*, Sherman is quoted saying in *Veronica's Revenge: Contemporary Perspectives on Photography*. Consider the metaphorically material development Acker makes to be seen in one of her titling moves. From George Bataille's *Story of* to her *Portrait of*—and from *the* to *an*—less rarified? *Eye.* My pen, my typewriter, my computer, my paper, might be made equally mediumistic, as might any book. In "Requiem," the character Acker puts through the paces of her life story this time is named "Electra." Mythical, culturally-preserved plotter of the mother murder is called upon by stage directions to be seen *shutting her book which she never goes anywhere without—it doesn't matter which one.*

89.

To ground anew experience reading, we can work back to an earlier pondering like one of the dear Alice: *What is the use of a book without pictures or conversations?* Interviewed by Acker for *Bomb* magazine about his film *Motive*, Michael McClard says, "You know all those kings of narrative conventions. Like the way language is used to close the plot, in order to make it hang together..." The Traveler's Digest publication of *I Dreamt I Was a Nymphomaniac: Imagining* published in 1980 contained drawings by him: a peep-show window marked "Teller," a woman on her back with legs spread and knife in her hand tipped to one buttock. McClard also illustrated Acker's 1982 chapbook, "Hello, I'm Erica Jong," writing folded-in for the novel of *Blood and Guts in High School*, where it undergoes a few changes, temporal and typographical. Some things become all-caps, and some running sentences become regulated with periods. Like: *MY NOVEL CONTAINED REAL PEOPLE. THAT'S WHY YOU LIKED IT.* "Oh, yes" loses its comma, an instance of *googoo* gains a dash. An *I* divides the line: *I AM ERICA JONG I FUCK ME YOU CREEP.* Six paragraphs before are formatted three. It gains in its conclusion some graphic approximation of handwriting, the signature of the author Jong. McClard's drawings are not reproduced here or in the *Portrait of an Eye* gathering of *The Adult Life of Toulouse Lautrec*. I am perhaps projecting, but does the author try to make the hand script thinner, a bit taller, slightly more reserved—scratchy, even— than the other reproduced in the same novel to key maps of dreams and to give directions to other images Acker provides, or that mocked-out composition of "The Persian Poems" by Janey Smith, protagonist largely in *Blood and Guts in High School*?

90.

As the line of drafting is moved and forced and allowed to evolve, Acker works the lines of prose, the lines of the talk coming at her, too, in the interviews. Again I go back to the one with Lotringer, who reminds her of a time she planned to go sailing around the world, pleasure cruising the high seas, like Jordana in Harold Robbins's *The Pirate*, or the Durasian female loner in *The Sailor from Gibraltar*, one of Acker's two favorite books by the vanguard writer. *Le Ravissement de Lol V. Stein* is the other. Acker places both Duras titles on a "le recit" reading list she draws up. There is a rumor that Alexandria is a place where their criminal man might be in *The Sailor of Gibraltar*. She calls upon *Le Ravissement* as example in the introduction she contributes to a book on "Boxcar Bertha": *Nowhere to run. Nowhere to hide, but, like Marguerite Duras's Lol Stein, in the lack of self. Or, like Boxcar, keep on travelin', Girl.* (The introduction is *for my friend Melissa*, Acker appends inside parentheses to the essay's conclusion.) If cuts exist in interviews for her, they are from the literal to more metaphorical expansion. She trails off in answer to Lotringer, "Yeah, but we didn't know how to sail...," "I guess I just want to go on a journey and so I start with a sentence and then the language twists and turns and you don't even remember where you've been, you're always faced with the present."

91.

Acker's work is of the epistolary, with a more general, expanding address: a gathering in from further corners, a self-selecting world. Those who will: fall in line. They will have to try to find her, the real "her." PORTRAIT: *My sex operates as a mask for my need for friends.* Books did this for me and some of you I'm sure. PORTRAIT: *I have to stop acting like I'm shy.* In a section marked "Addendum," to one of the letters part of the second chapter of *My Mother: Demonology* ("Letters from My Mother to My Father"): "If you want to contact me, you'll have to find me. / If you really know me, you can do this." The artist Nayland Blake is resonant for me, writing in *Lust for Life* of her books, "I read them like they were letters written to me." I read her books in a small town as a poet keeping a diary. One correspondent refers hopefully and gleefully, as I read it, to a recently received piece by her as "the latest episode in the flesh war." I respond to the credos running throughout her approaches to writing. One *Nympho* correspondent calls the work "investigations," another, "A handbook how-to maybe...specializes in the present, stroking it over and over with repetition. Reminds me a little of Huysmans' A REBOURS which goes over & over various forms of man-made reality." Acker herself talks about the "Tarantula" work as a process; in brainstorming a future collaboration and one way to go about it, "as I read your stuff do a TARANTULA on it (since that's how I read carefully)."

92.

The Black Tarantula corresponds with Kenneth Rexroth and Bernadette Mayer. Mayer writes, "New book great but make em longer!" Titled out as inventory of Mayer's papers, part of the offerings Acker sent are "Records of Daily Life" and "A Map of My Dreams." The Jackson Mac Low papers show a copy of "RipOff Red: Girl Detective" was sent to him in 1973. Ron Silliman believes he remembers Acker having birds named Jackson Mac Low and John Cage. A calling card she had prepared resembles in ways those drawn in Chance or Community Chest in a Monopoly game: an asterisk ideogram sprouts in relaxing, concentrating hand elongating, curling legs, this way and that reaching out and bending from a central design, to create perspective. Accompanying script alleges, "You are on the enemy list of The Black Tarantula." She signs her contribution to the October 1979 issue of L=A=N=G=U=A=G=E magazine, dedicated to the politics of poetry, featuring also work by Terry Eagleton, Michael Palmer, Hannah Weiner, and others: "Miss Criminal."

93.

In the spirit of extension and complement, Acker's *Great Expectations*, in part an unwrapping and re-parceling of Dickens, will not confine itself only to putting Peter in the Pip place: *My father's name being Pirrip, and my Christian name Philip, my infant tongue could make of both names nothing longer or more explicit than* Peter. Or (Peter) Gordon in Mr. Jaggers's place: *My lawyer Mr. Gordon duly sent me his address; and he wrote after it on the card 'just outside Alexandria, and close by the taxi stand.'* It plays as well with Proust: "During our walks together, Gilberte talked to me about the way Robert was losing interest in her and increasing his attentions to other women." On the same page: *During our many walks together, Peter's new girlfriend Shang-shi talked to me about the way Peter was losing interest in her and increasing his attentions to other women.* Like Peter with the women, Acker begins to lose her interest with the source with which she began. She moves onto others, a child playing with blocks, building different sets and houses, different "environments," and moving back and forth between them. LECTER: "I wanted to do some sort of environmental writing, the way Bob Ashley was doing environmental music." So she "started doing my version of GREAT EXPECTATIONS, cutting it up, not even rewriting, just taking it and putting it together again, like playing with building blocks." The model that arises need not necessarily have all or only four walls and windows where one might expect. In correspondence around the *Great Expectations* book, letters used to make and part of another book, *Spread Wide*, Acker saw another material aspect for writing, which could become an element of her own. She confides: *endless worries: you don't know what you're doing anymore kid you're off on your own process track no one will ever understand you're using language not language but given language, as in Flaubert's, like paint, now just given material, sculpting it.* Composed of the works of others, the Acker *Great Expectations* book would signal turns, showcase, fan out other authors within her sentences from theirs. For angled purposes of transport, the word, the book, is made more untransparent, becoming something else as progeny, as the material of the previous books is made anew in some current medium.

94.

Something could be made of an early refusal, in her Papers a gloss of that "stuff written during a part of my life I now hate and fear, so can't even read the crap to edit it, I'm scared of it. So it might be horrible (includes POLITICS)." To not revise is noted in some context, one developmental strategy, in an evolving work, her finding a way to continue moving forward through some of the initial stumbling blocks. Not looking back might be made part of a process. Up and flinging yourself into another field of concerns, chance then upon what might return. Beyond unfiltered transcription of first thought, slap-dash, much could be made equally of an eventual revision process. Both Peter Wollen and Leslie Dick share in this understanding and contribute it to the *Lust for Life* volume. Wollen: "Acker used to read her own texts too, each one eight times, re-drafting it after each reading—once for meaning, once for beauty, once for sound, once to the mirror to see how it looked, once for rhythm, once for structure, and so on." Dick, "Acker rewrote her texts eight times: once for sound, once for meaning, once for 'beauty,' once for structure, once in the mirror for performativity, etc...." How much more exhaustively I would like to be able to get us into those eight times—like training each of the spider's eyes, one at a time, back onto the composing— by knowing those last two missing criteria I cannot begin to imagine, trust I know. I do, though, believe it might be more easily pinpointed around where the regulated revision, displacing a regimen of obsessiveness, begins. It is right around the time of *Empire of the Senseless*, or with the next book, with that turn to the *making* of new myths, this rather than taking apart only all the old ones. An early manuscript markup by her of pages from *My Mother: Demonology* contains throughout it the notation in its margins "color," as if it must, or should, be added next time around. "Just say" is another, seeming to indicate a need to shift from the fictional overlay Acker would be currently engaged with to spelling out more subtext, in these cases apparently how the flown sentiments—of Laure, of Bataille—relate to Acker's own, actual life. *In Memoriam to Identity* comes between *Empire of the Senseless* and *My*

Mother and is "cleaned up," as she expresses it to Lotringer. It is much more narrative. "What I'm really interested in is this myth of romantic love."

95.

The walls of the novel open out, to hop along, ducking down one hole after the next. PORTRAIT: *This is an Alice-in-Wonderland room.* PASOLINI: *I remember mental states of Alice-in-Wonderland and the Caterpillar-on-the-Mushroom.* PUSSY, KING: *As if I was in Wonderland.* She runs into and through halls of mirrors of philosophy in writing, in that last title where it goes in bold: "Hegel, or the panopticon, sees all, except for the beginnings of the world." She goes on, sleep writing even. Carla Harryman is a preserve of this last anecdotal knowledge bit and co-editor of *Lust for Life: On the Writing of Kathy Acker,* the volume compiled from papers and talks from a weekend-long Acker symposium (New York University, 2002). Name misspelled, she is also a dedicatee of a section of Acker's *Pasolini* book, the "Narrative breakdown for Carla Harriman" section of the "Language" part of the "Nominalism" section. Acker with Friedman, of the book in general: "I think it's probably unreadable, but it fascinated me to write it." I will quote Robert Glück's covering of similar territory. "After *Empire of the Senseless* was finished, she said she was glad to sleep through a night again, since she had been waking herself up for months to write down her dreams." "In *Empire of the Senseless* she dreamt the plot forward." She either continues on with, comes back to, or fictionalizes the technique three books later, when it is written: '*I, King Pussy, see through my dreams...*' / *King Pussy had to masturbate to see this one:* /

'*I see two girls, can't distinguish all limbs, about to lose energy, dissolving, as if into gasps, hardly see figures.*' As she tells Laurence Rickels in *Artforum*, "The work with dreams comes out of the work with the body: you can't separate language and the body from the realm of the imagination." This stands in relation to *the real*. "Dreaming and masturbation are different techniques of writing." "And it's something everyone does; one doesn't have to desire to dream." To live and breathe through literature, that's Acker's territory. PORTRAIT: *if I again have to prostitute by becoming straight, is life—fakery of living—that necessary to me?* She will work to try to make in the text a place of more freed-up exchanges. We move both up and down, backwards and forwards, and in through—a fog of reasons: a subliminal skin: writing might be made to yield up, to provide, hold and, or, to cloak.

96.

Over time, a movement I see to begin already in the *Toulouse* work included in *Portrait of an Eye*, the Acker standalone book does progress towards involved coherence, increased intricacies. Though she tells Lotringer how *on the whole, friends* "can read wherever they want, at least up through DON QUIXOTE" she says: "Oh they're structured, they're carefully structured. There's always a beginning and an end." Then a kind of concession: "Well, to some of them. GREAT EXPECTATIONS has no beginning nor end, but there's cumulative effect." I admit here the emergence of an occasional, perhaps misplaced, aggression. I am in some days dissertating—investigating in the drifts between genres rectifying nothing, but struck by sensation of trying to pick through divine wreckage, or finding myself cleaning up after a child gone bananas in the playroom, throwing around there what is at hand. I do not leave it though.

97.

In writing on Blake with Blake, artist Nayland by the way of incorporating poet William, she uses an extraction the origin of which is hard to locate. In fact it is much to my delight when Amy Scholder wants to know if I know where it comes from. Nayland himself was wondering, as he was preparing to write on Acker's essay on him. In one of her pieces, Acker uses a version of this same mysterious story in writing about William Burroughs. Both the Burroughs piece and the Blake piece are dated 1990. In the "Burroughs version," it appears Acker is quoting a story of a friend, introduced into the essay, in an attempt to show how she works. She cuts-up the quote. This becomes clearer when one reads it again "quoted" again in the Blake piece, as it is shifted out of the quotation marks and retold this time in third person. There you can see how another passage becomes leveled onto the end of the earlier one. In the first version, the narrator walks into a kind of clarity, whereas in the second, an artist thinks through comparison, located upstairs and with a dream calling into realization a present. The dream used here is Nayland Blake's own, as told to Acker it turns out, a fact supplied by his eventual essay. For the most part, Acker allows herself to drift by now a long way from earlier days of fanciful, yet by all appearances accurate and complete, attempts at citation of sources from which the writing sprung that followed each of the units comprising *The Childlike Life of the Black Tarantula by the Black Tarantula*.

The only published book written as a novel in which such attribution would exist is 1990's *In Memoriam to Identity*, concluding, "Note: All the preceding has been taken from the poems of Arthur Rimbaud, the novels of William Faulkner, and biographical texts on Arthur Rimbaud and William Faulkner." Gone are days of trying to account for each and every one, days of "the above events (and thoughts) taken from," then a list of read and utilized crime books (e.g. *Enter Murderers!* by E.H. Bierstadt, *Blood in the Parlor* by D. Dunbar), historical accounts (*A Book of Scoundrels* by Whibley), plus "myself," "my past," "my fantasies," etc.

98.

Low was published on the occasion of a Nayland Blake exhibition at Petersburg Gallery, New York, 1990. It steps from an opening story, included in the Acker reader, on to further pages of essay given in *Bodies of Work*. It begins with a telling of Hansel and Gretel and ends with dead parents as independence. William Blake poems are dropped in, along the way, to the end. In its more elaborated presentation, there is a cut to Deleuze on cinema (specifically, Deleuze on Pasolini). Next presented by her are working definitions of "Innocence," "Prison," "Dream Sexuality Art" (non-binary, this amalgamation is further named by Acker "The Magic Woods" in a following parenthesis) and "Vision." The piece then concludes in a verbal portrait of one artist as an Orpheus trying to escape unconscious rehashing in a natural history museum, reanimated and teeming-full of ever-expanding phantasy come back to life, defying once again the easily caught taxonomy that cages. The images in the scene root from the dreams Blake supplied Acker with as she was in her gathering phase for this writing, hired to do the catalogue. In an original publication of the work (not the book of essays or reader), there are reproductions and plates of Nayland's art dispersed throughout and two 1844 engravings, not William Blake's, that proceed and follow Acker's writing around Blake's artwork, her wood and understandings now. We see pictures of Nayland Blake's work, assemblages behind frames, under glass bell jars, with titles such as "Hysterical Arrangement" (#2 and #3), "Come Armageddon" (Morrissey title, and using a brilliant poster of said star), "Transport #4 (slung)," and "Work Station #6 (envy)." The pieces utilize such materials as: aluminum, steel, wood, glass, plastic, webbing, wax, mallard wings, cloth, string, potpourri, sea sponge, video cassette, latex, ceramic, vinyl, tortoise, slate, and canvas. Going all the way back again to Burroughs and his favored adage, as quoted from Gysin, of how far behind painting writing lags, imagine the exponential regress if that analogy were struck now and updated with the plastic arts *incorporating* painting as part of an overall structure. New ways of seeing, new ways of believing, bound up between the covers of books. Acker curates these things for us to exclaim over we might otherwise not find collected, preserved. As we acknowledge the tactile, textile artist, as well we may the textual.

99.

The line some version of was espoused for most of Burroughs's long writing life, in 1974 he is lamenting in the book of interviews Lotringer collected and edited as *Burroughs Live* over writers "still, for the most part, stuck to a representational position, a position they haven't allowed themselves to get out of, where painters have been out of it for the last 60 years. I mean, no painter today could get away with pure representation in painting. And any writer who does anything else is accused of being unintelligible." Edmund White, in introducing his interview with Burroughs, believes, "Of the writers in the generation to follow the great moderns (Joyce and Stein), Burroughs was the only one in English to remain constant to their ideal of continuing experimentation." Susan Sontag—whom Acker enlists in *Great Expectations* "Rosa" to call upon to help her in making her way—deems fiction a "sluggish art," though she sees it eventually unable to "resist certain influences from other arts." Also in *Conversations with Susan Sontag*: "The aims of the postwar period reverted to a kind of moral, sociological reportage in the tradition of the nineteenth century." *A Susan Sontag Reader*: "The difficulty arises because so many critics continue to identify with prose literature itself the particular literary conventions of 'realism' (what might be crudely associated with the major tradition of the nineteenth-century novel)." Burroughs portrayed the "psychotic realities" which Acker then saw, or sees in her 1990 essay on him, as the present, contemporary landscape. Sontag does go to the mat for Burroughs, among others, more than once. "For examples of alternative literary modes, one is not confined only to much of the greatest twentieth-century writing—to *Ulysses*, a book not about characters but about media of transpersonal exchange, about all that lies outside individual psychology and personal need; to French Surrealism and its most recent offspring, the New Novel; to German 'expressionist' fiction; to the Russian post-novel represented by Beily's *St. Petersburg* and by Nabokov; or to the nonlinear, tenseless narratives of Stein and Burroughs." Such an expansion of literary possibilities as this, here Acker would be conceivably home.

100.

In line with the great moderns, to follow them, in light of them, work through and around them, Acker settled into the experimentation as a way of life. In so doing, she not only wanted literature that was moving forward, but she also wanted to mark this to degrees as an issue from many paths and pasts. One notebook in her archive, named by her: "Ulysses Backward." Experiments may develop and change, complicate, rework themselves among themselves and others. That mythic man would surface again in *My Mother: Demonology*. The narrator there clarifies for the reader: *To go beyond. / This sounds romantic—actually I don't care if I have any mastery. I've no mastery of myself. I'm crumbling. I used to believe that I must understand and realize everything that constitutes me... and on this journey of realization, I came upon, just as Ulysses must have done, a monstrous cacophony. / I had no Penelope.* Original ellipses. Earlier in this book, in a chapter before, Penelope is used more directly against the narrator's idea of self that might emerge: *Why wasn't I more like Penelope? Penelope was polite, well mannered...whereas I...I understood the real message clearly: I should become less than nonexistent.* These thoughts go through a head while a mother is there in the background yelling.

101.

The loose narrator writes in the "longing for better things" section of *The Adult Life of Toulouse Lautrec*, "'You know that city called San Francisco.... I want to go there, Vincent. I love this American poet Ron Silliman who lives in San Francisco." Silliman is a real dispenser before the biographies of little-known facts of Acker and her movements in her earlier years, still around during my writing of this. Thursday, February 23, 2006: "Kathy Acker once did a piece that consisted of sending three of her current & former lovers to discuss her." He begins his blog entry for Saturday, December 14, 2002, matter-of-factly, "Of the 4,000 volumes of avant & post-avant writing I have lying around the house, none—not even the Clay Fear collection of Acker imitations with the blow job on the cover...." I underlined that "imitations," right away. A photograph on the cover of the Fear publication: a spectacular phallus, erection shot up from below, reproduced in black-and-white newspaper grain. With pronounced vein the image takes up all the volume's front. But when the publication is spread, opened facedown, a bigger picture is seen stretched over the larger space, moment in time now discernable, binding fold having halved an illustration, the rest of the story on the back, once prominence gets turned over, the piece all along having been anticipating consumption in the rest of the message of a woman's mouth.

102.

The third part of the *Portrait of an Eye* gathering, *The Adult Life of Toulouse Lautrec by Henri Toulouse Lautrec* holds for me a distinctive place within a consideration of the development of narrative in Acker's work. By the time of *Toulouse*, a story goes, too many people wanted the Tarantula pieces for her to continue going about production as she had in the past. The next work is created with a heightened, certain demand for Acker's writing in place already. She is no longer working under the measure of anonymity. Acker is granted financial backing through Sol Lewitt. LECTER: "Sol went to Ted Castle and Leandro Katz—Ted is an art-critic and Leandro a filmmaker—and he said he wanted to print these texts as real books. He basically became my patron." I notice she does not use the word novels. This, I believe, has implications for the larger plot. *Toulouse* is not constituted in segments individually first finished and then distributed before further work under some current, ongoing design of experiment proceeds. Also, *The Adult Life* adds to the identity explorations of the first two projects in the trilogy—and back into Acker's writing— the idea of the detective at first left behind in her somewhat abandoned, filed-away *Rip-off Red*. In the girl detective work, "Red" is trained in "the Sherlock Marlowe School for Private Eyes." She would investigate where Sally's father disappeared to every night at 10:00 P.M. for three or four hours. This time, though, a shift in the agency, no girl. The unsuspecting reader might hope, might feel invited or provoked to believe that there might be some solve here in or through *Toulouse Lautrec*. Opening the book and "The Case of the Murdered Twerp": *Poirot'll figure everything out. He's my father.* Where *The Childlike Life* opens with the roll call of births, *I Dreamt I Was a Nymphomaniac* with boredom as horniness, these the dynamics that set into motion the two evolving lines of flight, a narrative apprehended if at all by how one settles a relation of one lay of events to the next, how stringently, or creatively, one searches for a rationale organizing roped-off together distinctive spaces or how pleasurably one floats in between, arranges, stacks or collapses these instances of "I" within one's imaginative stores, we follow more clearly along for a time with the mystery design in *The Adult Life of Toulouse Lautrec*.

103.

Leslie Dick tells a story at the *Lust for Life* symposium of how Acker had lovebirds, pronouncing "parrots" in a way that always sounded to her as parents. Acker calls the Beats the "grandparents" of herself and the artists of her generation. Intensifying for herself Ginsberg's maxim, which she claims to be citing, she remarks upon his *First breath, best breath* in a piece in her papers, "An Actual Institution of Art." She recasts instruction in terms that remove any trace of a mind-body split: for his "thought," her "breath," an action arguably even more primary, even less mediated and meditated. Thoughts take the forms they come in. Potentially, she is also packing two Ginsberg ideas into one, given another adage of his of a line's length as dependent on natural speech rhythm, as it is tied to breath. From the page to the bloodstream by way of throat and lungs. Just as she branches in limns in Olson's poetic field, beyond the page to reliefs of other arts and an individual body's difficulties in consciousness navigating such God-given worlds.

104.

When I get in touch with Ron Silliman, I am told Clay Fear was Christopher Berg, a classical pianist by profession. I am warned also how there is more than one Christopher Berg in the professional music world. The one I am looking for has set the work of Frank O'Hara, Gertrude Stein, Nabokov, and poet Tim Dlugos to music. And that "wrong" one? Eerily, or not so surprisingly, given Acker's increased concern over time with the particular myths that can be said to suffuse our culture, still seems right in some light as the composer of a piece inspired by Orpheus and Eurydice. The Greeks are a particular cultural capital all their own. In *Pussy, King*: "Everybody knows that Orpheus, or O, or Or, was the most famous poet who's ever existed in all of human memory, or Greek memory, which soon might not be remembered anymore...." My ellipses. "'What about Eurydice?' Now I remembered. That was the name of Orpheus's girlfriend." "'He lost Eurydice 'cause he was ignorant: he never knew who she was, just like we don't know who Eurydice was.'" Before this book, *In Memoriam to Identity*: "Quentin was Orpheus. He knew if he looked back, he was going to die. Looked back at whom? He didn't remember. Maybe a woman. So a writer has to be fucking alone, he said, not to a novelist, he avoided novelists for the ambitious poseurs they are and hated their literary talk. A writer has to be alone because if he really touches anyone, which must involve looking back, he dies. But to be a great writer, you have to perceive. So: you are playing with death."

105.

In some of its dimensions, the *Toulouse* book becomes clearly patterned on Agatha Christie's *Hallowe'en Party*, where unattractive children were painted to have, unfortunately, fallen under the sway of corrupting elders, and underneath the artistic temperament is found to be lurking an evil character. The murder mystery that Mrs. *Ariadne* Oliver and Poirot combine talents of deduction to work out Acker has a compositional pairing of her Toulouse-Lautrec and his friend in Van Gogh take in. A girl's body is found facedown in a tub of bobbing apples. "Do you always bob for apples? Whose idea was that?" The detective, like the whore, is an idea that would insistently come around again in Acker. As late as *Pussy, King of the Pirates*, Acker begins with this functionary entering: "O went to a private detective. He called O a dame." The narration designation of this character: private eye. PUSSY, KING: "I'm looking for my father."

106.

One I read as a child, *Hallowe'en Party* is an effort Christie critics find disappointing, but here is my keenness on its appropriation. Christie's reusing of themes and old devices were felt by critics to be more clunky here in her trotting them out. Acker speaks of "resting," in her *Toulouse* book—not pushing herself forward in terms of her "I" experiments, to some degree perhaps luxuriating in what had already been found. This basic assessment is in ways ungenerous. The book would anticipate many of Acker's later, and more involved, novelistic moves. Within the case of *Toulouse*, Acker begins to thread earlier "Tarantula" projects through a larger structure for narrative— not quite an arc, complete with that expected, traditional climax, one that does eventually yes collapse, but she is clearly composing links across first chapters with resurfacing characters and a fledgling plot in and through something like a mystery. The whorehouse setting proves to be an expansive base for narrative, spawning not just the murder but artists—"whores" for comforts—and their further stories told: a "history lesson" we are given in chapter three, or an exposition of how Vincent Van Gogh got to be so low ("the desperation of the poor," as Acker titles this ration); "Marcia/Janis Joplin," of the book's second generation, daughter of Vincent "and a clap-ridden sleaze-hag prostitute Vincent fell in love with in The Hague around 1881," issues also from the domain of body commerce. Despite this novel start, though, it is really only a matter of time before *The Adult Life of Toulouse Lautrec*, and its nested, budding narrative development Acker began proceeding to involve, slides back toward the wholly more procedural ends of *The Childlike Life of the Black Tarantula* and *I Dreamt I Was a Nymphomaniac*. In the final movements of *The Adult Life*, Acker has allowed the bottom to completely drop out of the propelling investigation, forgets it. It appears we are now charting an evolving Hollywood Romance (between James Dean and Janis Joplin or "Marcia") before the Dean/Scott and Joplin/Marcia story gives way or metamorphoses into "the life of johnny rocco." It concludes: *They weren't even going to kill me. I ran out of that warehouse. I had no idea where to go. I kept on running.* "I" is back now in its vintage regalia. Hardin cites the *Rebel Without a Cause* chapter in *Toulouse* as the first clear instance of Acker's "plagiarism," a distinction that seems to indicate a text which Acker does not rewrite to any marked degree but just places in, as she does with stretches of dialogue from scenes of the movie. Between transcriptions of the film's dialogue, Acker provides an editorializing and synopsizing commentary. The books of the *Portrait* work conclude when a given constraint, its endeavor, has run its course for Acker. An end is marked, eliciting the need somehow for a new title or a new series.

107.

Against the *lobotomy, the shits, the robot, the creeps,* Acker posits desire in imagining, her formulating of other possible agency. Against a "robot" can be written the muscles as they awaken during sex and move. Self and other, subject and object, high and low, literature and pulp, love and body, she wants these to turn over; isolation taken down by love, the contained or open-ended, holy and debased, East and West, beautiful and ugly, the vertical and horizontal, organized and scattered organic, standing-up and lying down, the writer erected, reader, creator, receiver—*enlightened* models butt heads with notes more based instinctual. Acker will move forward within binary couplings, when she does, to make more wrenchingly apparent their interdependence, their mutual supports, to un-dam exchange and allow for the making of a: *more.* Roland Barthes decides on under the heading of "The goddess H." *the pleasure potential of a perversion*: "perversion, quite simply, makes happy; or to be more specific, it produces a *more.*" His emphasis. Too much for me to try to hear, here, love in another tongue? In Rimbaud's "H," in his *Illuminations*: "Erotic mechanics, her solitude; her lassitude, amorous dynamics." Of the Rimbaud piece, critic and translator Wallace Fowlie writes, "He defines elaborately with an eye to mystification and a will to deliberately obscure." In the fragment "The Cuttlefish and its ink," Barthes writes, "I am writing this day after day...I tie up my image-system (in order to protect myself and at the same time to offer myself)." These processes I find applicable to Acker, too.

108.

Within the hands of Acker I find myself, admittedly, somewhat passive. She has her guiding lights for thinking, and she plays her own games. She follows along, setting down what occurs to her along the way, through their words, exposures, to them. Along with her, this becomes permissive relief. The Black Tarantula says, "I'm not interested in what I, except as a medium, have to say." I do not doubt Acker means here too, through her, that word to be heard as a body bridging the land of the living and of the dead. An *I*: the idea of any stable identity becomes for Acker the field to derange or rearrange, the constituent points and poles of which can and might be moved and refigured, for a number of pages. My own set "I," it logically follows, welcomes these windings through the sides of the self. A utopian, for me, incarnation: to have the reader of this here increasingly relaxed into quotations and fewer periodic assertions, more and more. I might feel myself less called upon to declare some worth with the punctuation of my own claims.

109.

Acker held her childish belief that other poets, if real poets, would simply understand and see and accept what she was trying to do through her work, everything for which it stands. *In Memoriam to Identity* includes: "Ode To A Drunk Fly (in the Tradition of Landscape Poetry)," "Poem in the Tradition of The Poet Maudit," a category of creator she identifies with in her McCaffery interview, broaching Kristeva, *Powers of Horror*. There are poems consisting of Acker's own translating— "copping"—of Rimbaud's poems, and other untitled pieces harder to place on first glance. Pointedly much of Acker's work must be. I would extend "work" to winding her way through publishing venues, organs, and institutions open and available to her, never just stopping there.

110.

Often from far-flung sources, the sentences of the books would be arranged into one book together over the page conceived in spatial dimensions. With their headings and titled interrupts, more marked-off areas would be caused to be perceived fields of storied critiques to be experienced set off in sections where and of: "The Beginning," "On The Street," "The Gritty State Of Things To Come," "Animality," "I Journey To Receive My Fortune," "The Beginnings Of Romance," "Portrait In Red," "The Underworlds Of The World." I sample just a few of the narrative posts in *Great Expectations*. I am in some agreement with McCaffery, who goes so far as to classify Acker's works *'prose assemblages' (to refer to them as 'novels' misses the point)*. To refer to them as "novels," I believe, creates another. Like a sculpture with panels of paintings set in relative reliefs, walls of her own constructed reflections are the only ones she wants to find herself up against. PORTRAIT: *A few inches from my body I create a wall of bricks white concrete that exactly mimics the contours of my body I'm tough as possible.* The walls we'll keep coming back to, as Acker tries to reshape not only them, but also, in response, the body of a book. Putting her life into the frame and among the words of stories in the books of others, to see what of it they might hold, Acker reworks the use to descend from them and situate herself. In another *Spread Wide* letter, she identifies how an underlying thematic in the character of pieces she will pull from to compose her own will set structure rolling, staking Propertius "leads of course into Nietzsche because he too was up against the wall." On no fronts in Acker will the single master text exist.

111.

She tells McRobbie that David Antin, whom Acker classifies as a poet and an art critic and one of her main teachers, told her that if you want to be a writer you have nothing to do with academia. In *The Burning Bombing of America* is where it was decided: *writing is the use of information without the source of the information.* But this is not to say that Acker does not at times cite sources, like in her essays. Though, "I question the works you're about to read," she writes in preface to a volume of them. And: "I'm not sure I like my essays." Attribution is a sporadic praxis with variable intents. It is not a process to ever completely stand behind, or leave uninflected ironically. For example, take footnote three of "Reading the Lack of the Body: The Writing of the Marquis de Sade," where to substantiate the fact that his Madame de Saint-Ange has in twelve years of marriage slept with 12,000 men, we are directed to a bolster of cross reference: "Note de Sade's realistic tendencies." PORTRAIT: *getting a straight job would lobotomize me a wall breaks down.* A piece titled "The Black Tarantula interviews David Antin 12/28/73" is playing exchange as conducted through or taken from ON CERTAINTY by Wittgenstein and "self." (I add the inflection.) Speculations include whether or not Antin wants to sleep with the interviewer, before she signs off: "All love to David," and I imagine goes back to babysitting.

112.

Acker was, one disputed rumor has it, tutored by Herbert Marcuse ("radical neo-Freudian emphasis on the role of eros in politics," is how Wollen sums up this one luminous enough to lie about). A detail of how she traveled early on for him is propagated. Acker, studying classics at Brandeis, when he left his position to become a Professor at the University of California, San Diego, follows. She was his TA, or she sat in the back of the class. There she would meet that other man, David Antin, one half of a mentoring couple. She seems to have had the propensity for inserting herself among such units. Leslie Dick at *Lust for Life* spoke of how Acker would introduce Dick and Peter Wollen, partnered at the time, as her parents. Carla Harryman and Barrett Watten, paired and with their own interests in her work, were also prominent in the *Lust for Life* production. The Acker letters to Paul Buck began initially addressed to both him and his companion at the time. It is a while before Acker begins to write the two of them separately. First, *Dear Paul, / Just wrote Glenda and in a letter put some pertinent info like forwarding addresses future plans so can she give you the info so I don't have to repeat? I AM being tacky.* Then: *If it's O.K.—only if it's O.K. cause I know you are different people—show this letter to Glenda—only cause I've poured my heart out (a bit) & now am (a bit) tired yet want to say hello to Glenda I miss you too.* "New York City in 1979" is called fiction. Acker writes how Janey yawns, although: *she doesn't fall asleep cause she's suddenly attracted to Michael who's like every other guy she's attracted to married to a friend of hers.* A boyfriend I had, a poet, brings to my attention this reference, "...elly and i / we were sitting by watching kathy acker die [ ] she was a dear friend of ours and an ex-student [

] someone we really loved and we watched her die young and terribly of cancer [ ] and what do you do in those circumstances [ ] sitting there you do the best you can," *i never knew what time it was*, Antin.

113.

Once there in San Diego where Marcuse is now Professor at the University of California, Kathy babysits for the Antins. Chris Kraus writes to Dick that Eleanor Antin is someone whom Kraus doesn't know much about. Antin is recognized in Peter Wollen's contribution to *Lust for Life* as providing "a role model for Acker as a female performer and avant-gardist, one of the first women to make her mark as a conceptual artist." Some see how modes of Eleanor's practice could be reduced to blackface, no matter how deeply she tries living these roles. There have been some critiques. Acker learns from her mentors, real and imaginary. Eleanor designed, painted, costumed, choreographed, wrote and performed. One of Eleanor's exhibitions, 1973: *I Dreamed I Was a Ballerina*. Eleanor*a* Antino*va*, "celebrated Black Ballerina of Diaghilev's Ballet Russe," is one such creation, with her piece "Before The Revolution." While she still hasn't settled her identity, Kathy writes the bits that can be worked into the sustaining of the *I Dreamt I Was a Nymphomaniac* project. An entry in an early Acker notebook records how Eleanor told her to start sending her writing out, to begin the mail art that is the identity trilogy eventually. In fact, Kathy uses the same contacts Eleanor had for the disseminating of *100 Boots*. In an Acker piece, David and the charge, young Blaise (Jackson Mac Low's "22nd Light Poem," "For David Antin & Eleanor & Blaise Antin") are imprisoned and treated harshly by a penal system for being "agitators," thus possible "revolutionaries," alongside the "dykes" this stretch or chapter is named after, punished along with a string of prisoners classified as "Adjustment Center candidates." Militants are targeted. So are the seen-as-weak. Eleanor comes to Acker's defense when the charge seems lodged apparently from one corner (B. Mayer's) that Acker's *poetry* is "didactic." Correspondence*: As if that were a put-down instead of the reasonable behavior of an intelligent artist living in the U.S. in 1974.* Urgent, passionate, expressive support becomes more important than spelling, as I go about correcting here typos. (Like Acker putting "i" before the "e" repeatedly in *weird.*) In a pre-*Childlike* work, begun in notebooks labeled "Jane Eyre," all caps: NO MORE CHANING FROM FIRST WRITING DOWN. In *The Burning Bombing of America,* recording, already anticipating; *friends disappear appear betray me.*

114.

As one way to pursue what proves to be a lifelong interest in the intersections between classics and philosophy—a philosophy that becomes increasingly cultural and queer—she would begin but not complete post-graduate work at what was to be my alma mater, the City University of New York. I see this documented abstractly, no dates, in numerous sources. It proves difficult to be more clearly responsible about, especially given paper records, as one administrator attempts to move me along with, compounded by the numerous permutations of Acker's names: given, chosen, adopted, modified. She signs a letter to the man she believes to be her father, once she tracks him down: "Kathy (Alexander) Acker/ (Karen Lehmann)." The letter is in her

Papers. Chris Kraus has a PI friend who might help her track down a few facts. Someone I talk to in a records office suspects whatever undertaken degree was probably through City College. Various other sources list Acker as an alumnus of New York University. Some cite her post-graduate work as a joint degree undertaken between The City University of New York and New York University. In *The Burning Bombing of America*, in the section "Information Sexual Ecstasy Revolution III," this lexia, jibe, this jab—appears: *CUNY-Nixon headquarters explode.* In this dream or perfomative, however premature, I find a note of Gertrude Stein's famed, "Dear Professor James, I am so sorry, but really I do not feel a bit like an examination paper in philosophy today," be it less so mannered.

PART TWO
I, 0, & You

It would be futile to try to separate out materially works from texts.

Roland Barthes

1.

Acker, like a child wandering, attempts to leave home, school, and this world as it is most commonly known, as it's been so far structurally defined and classified. "New York City in 1979": "What has usually been called the world is the male world." One must leave that, she sees, make leaves of it, hay made to find the self home. She might call out from the stacks just for an echo: the mark, oh. Bales. *My Mother*: "I remember that I hid among these books for a long time." MOTHER: *In this place, Miss St. Pierre, who looked like my mother except she wasn't beautiful, showed me books to read. Melville and Keats, Yeats and a battered* The Wizard of Oz."

2.

In one of her last works, "Eurydice in the Underworld": *Clean white bandages curve around the torso from below the armpits to the bottom of the rib cage*, she writes, making a metaphor of her present condition and life around it in Orpheus and his other half. Also from the year of her death, in *Requiem* she writes matter-of-factly how: *Then the surgeon took my breasts off.* In a version even more scaled-down than the one eventually collected, it is published in *The Guardian* as the final piece she wrote before she died, an excerpt only in fact, composed of Scene 1 and the end of the final scene of Act Three (Scene 2). Though these pieces were signed by Acker and released, both the works from this year feel to be in all likelihood only the cordoned-off parts of a vision foreshortened. Viegner gives in his memoiristic piece "Cannibal Acker" how she told a healer she was working with, "she never really liked her breasts and was happy to look like a boy."

3.

After all the births that take place in the first movement, or chapter, of *The Childlike Life of the Black Tarantula* piece, we read forward if being the good Westerners we have been taught to be, but Acker displays truck with this in development. PASOLINI: *Probation school at least taught excuse me trained her to act normal.* We watch the *I*'s of the books multiplying before our very own and we come up with our strategies to try to contain them or give in, move in a flight forward, borne into different circumstances, other possible identifications. PORTRAIT: *I'm born crazy in Barbican, four years after the defeat of the terrible Armada.* The reader is set up, prompted by an invitation to inquiry on a back cover of *The Childlike Life* when given its first publication with the TVRT Press: *In Troy, New York, an Irish bartender and his wife's sister are brutally murdered... / A tidal wave of thievery and terrorism hits London... / A young girl is found with cut-up wrists on the corner of Fifth and First Avenue in New York City...* As we get with other books with Acker, the attempt is made to proceed less reined-in, less singularly. We get also on that back after a space, "I wake up and can't remember anything. / Blood lies inside my legs. Have I gone crazy? / Am I a murderer..." In the Serpent's Tail/High Risk Archive, a manuscript of an unpublished 1977 work by Acker, "For the Ladies Who Sing: Three Stories," includes a note to self to insert "List of Murderesses." Among those same papers, a title page of what she marked as "performance copy" of her "New York City in 1979" reads (crossed out eventually): "anything that destroys limits." *Rip-off Red, Girl Detective*, like *The Childlike Life*, features a collection of alter egos. Some repeat between the two works: Henriette Cailloux, Lizzie Borden, Jane Cannon

Cox, Florence Chandler Maybrik, Lydia Danbury Sherman, Madeline Hamilton Smith, Maria Marten, Adelaide Blanche de la Tremouille, Mary Ann Cotton. What do all the women share? They become other than well-adjusted to the society that they have been brought into and then asked to live in. They go then to murderous lengths, either to take up for their husbands or to get away from their husbands, because they aren't getting enough money or because someone's going to kick them out, or to stop a husband's misery, or stop kids from suffering, because the child is illegitimate, or because they need money, or because now, "he wants to fuck her first time ever 11 years marriage," or because he won't marry her, or for reasons we can't understand, because someone raises a Union flag, because everyone denies her.

4.

While one of her first, more distinctive textual moves had been the construction of her many-I-ed narrators, the main points of reference significantly drifting, that I floating gives ways in later books to interactions with third-person stretches as well. The opening framework of *The Adult Life of Toulouse Lautrec by Henri Toulouse Lautrec* has as its overarching conceit a signed-on success, a possession of a voice from the culture past coming back to speak in new word arrangements heightened in those vocabularies, lenses, of Acker's making, as would be seen with poet-director Pasolini aloud thinking-writing: "Did I ask to die? Was my murder a suicide by proxy?" In *The Adult Life of Toulouse Lautrec* begins a subplot too, of a role of Giannina's travails in the whorehouse, along with Van Gogh and Toulouse and all the other sex workers. PORTRAIT: '*Any man'll fuck me,' Giannina tells Veronique in total privacy.* It is this "total privacy" though that we as readers are granted the godlike ability to look in on, from the beds or armchairs of comfort, a bird's eye view by Acker into the brothel business, an ability to peep even further into the innermost desires by hearing through walls the words. Giannina wants an exchange, an understanding that would take place more than her usual "once or twice," a deeper relationship, and she goes on to complain of how shallow the connections are, "like fucking the men in the porno movies I'm in. And I get paid to fuck when I make movies.'"

5.

In *Rip-off Red*, precursor to her later Acker books, when sex ("Plan Number 1" as the scrappy gang of street kids we are following dub it) is moved into once realizing there is no way these fledglings are going to win, with so many there on the other side ("thousands of filthy disgusting chain boys")—it's The Tomatoes vs. The Banana Followers—we as readers rhythmically experience a simulation of live-flesh action: "start I again I relax enough to become." And: "I can hear his breathing grow harsher harsher." Scholder in her Editor's Note to the Acker reader guides, "What cannot be overestimated is the pleasure Kathy took in writing porn, finding the exactly right cadence and rhythm: using language, pushing limits, turning on." In approaching the *pornographic*, Acker wants to get her rhythm down, a timing, just right. She wants to hear that pulsing and relieved voice inside her ear, whispering, the breathing, over spectrums of developments. Acker is never in her rewriting doing porn films, no, though movies themselves aren't off-limits for her. Greta in *Queen Christina* is an ego ideal in *Kathy Goes to Haiti.* "I had just finished making *Salo,*" Pasolini says in the book she names after him. PUSSY, KING: "Just as if I were watching *Salo...*" When at a loss for some direction in the loaded, decisive tête-à-tête with her father boyfriend in *Blood and Guts,* "Janey" holds noirish *Gilda* (Rita Hayworth, 1946) in her mind, with its tagline: *There NEVER was a woman like Gilda!* Chapter five of *The Adult Life of Toulouse Lautrec by Henri Toulouse Lautrec* is to be dominated by *Rebel Without a Cause.* Janis and Jimmy go to a drive-in together on a date in the same work to see *The Sun Also Rises:* "I got this vision and it's driving me crazy. Like Zelda Fitzgerald," Janis says (Zelda, who, according to her biographer Nancy Milford, saw through the swaggering macho persona of a Hemingway to be clearly little more than posturing). IDENTITY: *Said something like he liked the movie* Something Wild; *she said, she didn't.* PORTRAIT: *In* Rebel Without a Cause, *Jimmy Dean plays himself.* One set of lit up images of *Wuthering Heights* she dreams from in *My Mother: Demonology* is revealed soon enough to be connected to the big screen, though, "I had no idea which version." Here, too, cinema is one of the ways she returns to Violette Leduc's *Thérèse and Isabelle,* first used by her in *The Childlike Life of the Black Tarantula:* "I have always wanted my dreams to be like that of childhood or of Radley Metzger's film of the book *Therese and Isabelle.*" No diacritics in source. Pulling from the original medium is also used to end the book *My Mother: Demonology.* Where Leduc's "I" sees herself reflected in the toilet water—*a reflection of my face before the creation of the world*—Acker's sees, "Above me, the roll of white toilet paper was covered with specks of black hairs... / It was a reflection of my face before the creation of the world." This extreme assertion gains a complex level of pathos developed through Acker's hand in large part due to increasingly common knowledge—established and reiterated across her oeuvre—that in Acker girls often come with mother figures in tow who have attempted to abort or deliver their children into a toilet, trying to wipe away the daughter, mistaking often labor pains for appendicitis—as some survivor reports. This wretchedness also bears comparing to Clay Fear's narration, where the speaking subject more brazenly asserts search for "self" in the toilets: *I write on the bathroom wall this place needs more faggots.* I stress Acker approaches what is deemed porn not because she wants to get to see more than she normally does. She expresses her misgiving with the usual limits of its specular imagination in fact in her writing on and in praise of David Cronenberg's motion picture realization of J.G. Ballard's *Crash*: "What interested me most was that, contrary and probably antagonistic to all porn conventions, the cock is not hard. Through sexual desire, both his own and that of his characters, Cronenberg has reenvisioned the dominant and always rigid phallus of the old king-must-not-die world as other, soft, another body part...." Also of importance in *Crash* is a desire for the body, even be that male, to be made more porous and penetrable. (Remembering Acker's early focus on madness in *The Childlike Life*, I latch onto how sanity is equated with sexual penetrability in another film, John Cameron Mitchell's *Shortbus*.)

6.

Portrait of an Eye brings together some of the work Acker wrote while her primary experiment was with what she would later have the words to call, in an essay written on Colette, a "non-Oedipal I." More generally, to Lotringer, "Well, meeting you changed me a lot because by introducing me to the French philosophies, you gave me a way of verbalizing what I had been doing in language." Her work never does give up what overrides to unify these first pieces, though it can be seen to relax its more mathematical, gridded contours, further fenced in by the periodicity of dispersal. These works, like all of Acker's works, are meditations, mediated—on identity, eschewing or deconstruction of the reliability of the prop of singular, self-contained *I:* one. Acker never stops looking in her work, and through it—the work of looking through the works of others, for more open sites of exchange between versions of an "I," how it might exist over time, a way the exasperations might be skirted, to play around being something else. (Explaining a later technique to Rickels: *I literally stick a vibrator up my ass (up my ass! I mean up my cunt) and start writing.*) I contain multitudes, do I not, in one of the groundings of American poetics? 1980's "Fête," with an epigraph from Bataille's *Le Petit,* "...fête à laquelle je m'invite seul, où je casse à n'en plus pouvoir le lien qui me lie aux autres...," I might best describe as pamphlet or a broadside though folded. The text appears in a number of columns arranged around the lay of the page, and here self is equated with "the wound a kid gets on his knee all mushed up bottom-layer-skin blood dirt only all of me is this gush instead of the wound being in me so I am a fucked-up society."

7.

I falls back upon, into, history, back to the horizontal reclining in another book the better to look all around. *I* takes itself out of an always locked subject position, to create new being. The page becomes more leveled, the playing field, with obscurities and exposures patterned new through these old vantages. "The tree is in the wood," Juan Goytisolo tells Acker when she interviews him, I see in her papers. In an epigraph that John Yau uses for "Between the Forest and Its Trees (Second Version)," Jack Spicer says, "Where we are is in a sentence." In Acker, to take one particularly conducive example, where are we when we are in someone like Charlotte Brontë?

8.

We are in a set of shifting relationships. In a version of a sisterly one: Letters to Charlotte from Emily make up "CHILDHOOD: CATHOLIC BLATHERINGS" in the *My Death My Life* book. The correspondence you are presented with is one side of an exchange. A sample: "Dear Charlotte, 1968 is over. 1981 is over. Future is between my legs ha ha." You are in the hold of an allusion, as the world is seen in *Rip-off Red*: "the night is all around the red room." In "Eurydice in the Underworld": "The usual *Jane Eyre* shit." Ibid: *As my eye moved into the top floor of a house, it perceived that it was inside a school dorm. An immense room whose floor was wood. Narrow cots in rows covered the rough wood.* This is the "in the school of the dead" section, and "From Tsvetaeva: *It begins like a chapter in that novel* Jane Eyre. *The secret of the red room*," is in a "courtroom of the dead" section, italics in the original. *In Memoriam to Identity*: the character Father, in an argument with Rimbaud transposed now across time and space, uses a Charlotte example as authoritative grounds for knowledge of the opposite sex: *'You've never understood anything about women. She's not bad: she's sick. Women're always sick with wanting to eat up your soul. It's all in* JANE EYRE.' This narrator emphasizes, "Father read books," before turning to self: *I inherited his love of reading which proves that inheritance is important for human beings. A huge inheritance can make a miserable person's life happy.* Another way Brontë's bestseller enters the world in a book, in *My Mother*: "This room was the place I wanted to be." "It had no furniture, only the bed of *Jane Eyre*, which, of course, is wood, because it has been made out of wood from a building of the school that Jane Eyre attended." The "I" here has left school because, "All I wanted was to fuck and be fucked," and is investigating this new room for herself after a string of hotels.

9.

If she had her routine, as Burroughs did his, hers would be the dance, the strip of it words adhere through. A theatrical text, it carries its own dressing up and confusions of what is really behind what, where fantasy begins and ends. For one example, Santa Claus, as told to the "doctor" ("Politics"): *Santa Claus was going to bring me Christmas presents I couldn't go to sleep I was waiting and waiting and then and then you know what happened doctor Santa Claus came right into my room I'm taking my clothes my shoes off rubbing my breasts.* Cut to another work. In "Algeria," a character Hacene asks, "What do you and Santa Claus talk about, Miss Fendermast?" Omar answers back, "We don't talk at all. We play 'horsey' and 'doctor.' I like to play 'prison' best. It's new." Or, another routine: *I was a young wife last night....* We see it again in *In Memoriam to Identity,* in another instance: "Sex-show girl to sex-show guy: Doctor, I think I need a doctor. / Sex-show guy: I am a doctor"; "Having located her desires, the girl said, 'Doctor. I want Santa Claus'"; "'Santa Claus doesn't exist.' Now that the man had fucked her, he could show her what he really thought of her. The audience loved this one." The transposed scene, and this sense of Santa, first appears in *Politics,* predating Acker's mother's suicide occurring at a later Christmas time. Further grounding it, in a manuscript draft in her archive, Acker also identifies Christmas, symbolically, as a site of another or the ur-appropriation, that of winter solstice by Christianity.

10.

It was this work that kept me alive. Acker's expressed rationale in her determination of the writers she assigns pride of place, in an occasional piece, "Ten Out of Many Women Writers": *it's the writer's work throughout time, a life-time, the process rather than any individual work that interests me.* I could say much the same, vis-a-vis Acker. They might seem on the surface unlikely allies, but I do join her here to Susan Sontag, who argued for a similar sense of liminality. Take that case of Burroughs, for example. Sontag dropped his name often. In 1965's "On Style": "Until one has grasped, not the 'content,' but the principles of (and balance between) variety and redundancy in Merce Cunningham's 'Winterbranch' or a chamber concerto by Charles Wuorinen or Burroughs's *Naked Lunch* or the 'black' paintings of Ad Reinhardt, these works are bound to appear boring or ugly or confusing, or all three." How hard it is to tell someone which Acker book to start with, or point blank which one they should read if they have never read any. Sontag's thoughts on William S. go from, "At the time I wrote 'Against Interpretation' the new American writer who interested me most was Burroughs. He was the only writer who seemed to have broken some of the 'realist' stereotypes that limited American fiction," to, in 1987, amending in a piece collected in *Conversations with Susan Sontag*, "I was only seduced by some particularly salient formal aspects.... Reading Burroughs's subsequent fictions made me decide that I was mistaken about *Naked Lunch*.... If I'm at all engaged by somebody's work, whether it's a film, a dance, or a poem, then I always want to see or experience more of it." Sontag goes on: "Each part changes for me as I know more and more of the whole work, which means to know the work in a deeper way." We get to know parts of Acker's world situated through other characters. In her *Great Expectations*, "Rosa" simultaneously writes to and tries to write off those in, or not in enough, or not right enough in, her life: Peter, Sylvére, David, Mudd Club owner Steven Maas, God, and even Sontag. Though she is requesting Sontag's help to learn how to speak English, understanding that the critic is "very literate," Rosa proves quite conversant in some theories herself in her exchanges, among registers of nastiness and claims, acknowledgements of paranoia, frustration, delusions, and desperation. Summing up and referencing tenets of Jean Baudrillard's *Seduction*, Rosa tells Peter his new girlfriend is "only pretty because she's wearing a mask." Acker more nakedly elicits this name in *My Death My Life by Pier Paolo Pasolini*: "The separations between signifiers and their signifieds are widening. According to Baudrillard, the powers of post-capitalism are determining the increasing of these separations." This is before our boy poet, also called a brat, Rimbaud decries inside *In Memoriam to Identity*, "I'm sick of Baudrillard. The intellectual side of American postcapitalism. Cynicism." He is put into a poem Acker has "R" write: "Satan Triple-Master—cynic, money-hungry, pupil of Baudrillard." Back to *Great Expectations*: "Ours is the hottest love affair that has ever existed and I'm telling everyone that it is so." "Rosa," in further proposition, to Sylvére, "I think you should be nice to me because I'm just a helpless little girl." And: "I'm counting on you to help me out." Disgusting are the "half-artists the hypocrites the ACADEMICS who think it's in to be poor." Rosa goes on: "those CRITICS don't know what it's like to have to tell men they're wonderful for money," implying that she does. She asks David, "Are you a Tibetan monk yet?" She decides: "I should have stopped making demands that you not be the closet female-hating sadist you are." And: "Your explanation that you gave up writing your visions in order to do commercial Hollywood script writing because you needed Francis Ford Coppola's $150,000 when you receive huge monthly estate checks rivals a university professor's essay on the similarities between *Moby Dick* and Nazism. At least a university professor really has to make a living. Language means nothing anymore anyway." To God: "You are the world. I wish there was a man here who could put me back in touch with the world," signed, "Love, Rosa." After mentioning in passing how Sylvère fucks her, she then turns to and asks Sontag to please read Rosa and make her famous.

11.

I do not desire to exhaust Acker's output in my work in any way, critically or biographically. In response to a fear of not honoring adequately the complex of Acker's utterances, my handling it by attempting to straightjacket it in any ways, hoping I might find paths to allow it to speak itself more, a balance, Viegener supportively offered in a 2007 exchange, "It seems obvious to me (& was to K) that all interpretation is a form of appropriation, and there are no right or wrong forms to do that. More is better. It's not clear to me that KA's work is master-able, in fact I think it resists mastery both internally and externally, and I like that." We both do. I like when writing on her, like when reading her, I allow the bounce to pointed signs. I also see across her timeline, references and valences of repeating historical concerns. The Acker piece is never purely hermeneutically sealed endeavor—more often than not, it is far from being anything near that. The writing comes about from this move: what, when, where, how, why one might own—up to—how one might *spin* what has once been done, in writing, and too what one is about. With my committee I would discuss the possible use of the dissertation I would do. I pictured it as a kind of archive, but one that would circulate, might travel more. It had been a long time, if ever, since I was as happy as I was sitting among Acker's writerly effects at Duke, knowing there was so much I'd not seen, and more than I could ever want, or hope, to completely manage. I could still know things I hadn't known before. Little yellow Post-It notes were left behind by a worker there in those file boxes before me, dotted some of the folders, manuscripts, trying to put things more in order.

12.

Working with Acker can be difficult, if one wants to remain true to her spirit. As she opens "A Few Notes on Two of My Books," "If I had something to say about my writing outside my writing, something written which occurred outside my writing, my writing wouldn't be sufficient or adequate." But while a challenge of fidelity may exist, she also provides liberty, an example and the loophole. LECTER: *I use your work, you use my work, we use everyone's work.* As a critic, these leads I follow then working through her. Her job as writer becomes the collecting of errant pieces to handle, hold, to treasure, trove, spun turned over to further explore, move out into vaster possibilities for a meaning she comes to term as: wonder. One of her *languages of the body*, set out in her essay "Critical Languages," it stands in contradistinction to judgment. Others listed and qualified here would be: flux, contradiction, the material body's languages (laughter, silence, screaming), scatology (its own kind of laughter), poetry's playing power (absolutes broken down, with Pasolini a study in his chosen dialect), those that announce themselves as insufficient, intensities (sexual and emotive), those that given over to chance, encounter. "Seeing Gender": *I want to live forever in wonder.* And here is where one could begin to work in some earnest, with this concept. If I wanted to stress Acker's critical-artistic movement towards that Derridean, I would marry the state of wonder to his deferral, wander that close to a line. Acker claims in her interview with McCaffery, "Derrida was never as important," for her as Deleuze and Guattari and Foucault were. This is an enlightening interview, undated. I stress the articulation as one moment moving in time, or reading, outside of which particular fixations, fascinations, can be said to move on. Similar problems would exist with taking the intervention of the Lotringer essay opening *Hannibal Lecter* as gospel, more in circulation out there. While McCaffery's anthology released in 1996, and though a selected bibliography he includes cites 1993's *My Mother: Demonology* and 1996's *Pussy, King of the Pirates*, neither of these books enter into their discussion, discernibly peaking up around 1990's *In Memoriam to Identity*.

13.

A number of the essays Sontag wrote prior to *Great Expectations* would indeed do Acker's work great justice. Certainly Acker practices what might be called an erotics of art, as in "Against Interpretation," and I hope I might be able to here do the same in trying to read her, within her own preferences, her own oeuvre, and up against apparently unlikely bedfellows. Acker camps not only gender, but theories of it ("Notes on Camp"). This is not a dismissal of said theory, but it is a playing with it. In "The Pornographic Imagination," Sontag takes up both Bataille, under whose legacy the *My Mother* novel grows out, and *Story of O*, repeatedly surfacing in Acker's work. Of *O*, Sontag writes, "sexual arousal doesn't appear to be the sole function of the situations portrayed," obvious as well in a reading of Acker. They both deal with Artaud and a reverence of his values. He gains a characterization in *Pussy, King of the Pirates*, and he is a main point in Acker's speech for the "Artist In Society Conference," Chicago, 1994. They both point explicitly to Genet, work with and read Pavese ("The Artist as Exemplary Sufferer," Sontag), quote from *Endgame* (Acker uses a modified stretch of the Beckett in 1983's "Translations of the Diaries of Laure the Schoolgirl," where "Clov" becomes the "Maid"). There is shared appreciation for Jack Smith and Canetti. Acker's taking of her own cancer and fashioning the self, subsequently, through it in her last works as "Eurydice," makes a metaphor of not only physical plight but the conditions of a life surrounding it, makes both Sontag's "Illness As Metaphor" and "AIDS and Its Metaphors" relevant, as do Acker's notes on method to herself in writing "New York City in 1979," concerning the life of Baudelaire, and by extension Jeanne Duval: "THOUGH HE HAD SYPHILIS, THEN A PLAGUE, I'M ~~PRETENDING~~"—the crossout she replaces with *saying*—"THAT HE HAS AIDS." This document is in the Serpent's Tail/High Risk Archive, along with personal correspondence addressing her desire to clear the air, where Acker adopts terminology no less metaphorically loaded: "Too much festering these days." Another letter there, "Oh, it's probably the cancer making me grow up. Hard teacher?" The technological equivalent of a slip of the pen can be evinced as well. From home keys, rather than the left pinky punching down in place, going up with the right middle and giving that finger, before brought back down to rest among the others: *He's so mad he wouldn't know I coffin if he saw one.* I embolden here. Acker decides further: "I should put all that in the indicative sense." Given her case, Orpheus must be the lover in "Eurydice in the Underworld," if anyone is going to get her out. One way to go about reading Acker's *Empire of the Senseless* would be Sontag's "The Imagination of Disaster." Appreciation of Simone Weil represents for Sontag a "contemporary taste for the extreme in art and thought." *No one who loves life would wish to imitate her dedication to martyrdom....* Sontag places Weil in a line that includes, among others, some of Acker's true favorites: Baudelaire, Rimbaud, and Genet. "Some lives are exemplary, others not; and of exemplary lives, there are those which invite us to imitate them, and those which we regard from a distance with a mixture of revulsion, pity, and reverence." Then what does it mean that Acker has the figure of a mother register at a last hotel for impending suicide, "just as expensive, but newer, glitzier, for it caters solely to tourists," in this manner, "Will there be any luggage, Mrs.... (*looks down at the slip*)...Weil?" A typo in *Eurydice in the Underworld*? A letter dropped? A typo in the letter in her Papers? Acker typed to the man who may have been her father: "My mother is Claire Weill (Alexander) and I believe I am your daughter." Sontag sees in Simone Weil "contempt for pleasure and for happiness" and "ideals of bodily denial." It is the air of unhealthiness that creates the authority, as Sontag gleans it. Weil is Acker's mother, restrictive, who wastes away, denies herself nourishment, metaphorically culturally subtracting and ultimately a divine absence.

14.

Back in *The Adult Life of Toulouse Lautrec*, "I" at times is a whore double of a profit-driven creator, painting writer as love-maker-machine, threatening to eclipse Acker's own stances. She would differ in aiming to disrupt the dream of one size for all fantasies in such ways as she could, trouble a notion of continuity by pointing out from time to time a narrative hand might tip. There are other areas to consider. '*If you're nice to me and send me presents, especially money so I can get this trash printed,*' I exclaim, *rolling drunkenly over my matchstick legs, 'I'll tell you another story*, a story that will be "the true story of a rich woman," Jackie O. as amiss, as manhandled amidst the setup in Harold Robbins's *The Pirate*, restaged by Acker in Times Square.

15.

Transgression, or some "crime": the scenes are underlined in Acker's returning to again and again, like the spots lighting up an unprocessed, uncontrollable love, a love that wants to be kept, found: is that wanting. PORTRAIT: *I'm a mirror.* PORTRAIT: *I'm a cat.* PORTRAIT: "I want control over my environment. Like a fat spider I sit and wait. I float." I am not yet *Pussy, King of the Pirates.* I am not a woman or even a girl, not really. Not yet. Her understanding at one point of a Freudian model, as it is sketched out it in "Nice Girl, Gone Wrong 2," in her Papers and her underlines: _Things become sexual thru representation in fantasy_ / *Fantasy—(the sexualization)—no object-end: therefore can take any position in the fantasy.* Acker's own sentence is a modification of one lacking the noun-subject, as she reels out the logic chain. It is a proof illustrating a point in traveling through language. She is never just masturbating. PORTRAIT: "I begin to play with the spirals within me, my flames..." Interpretation has become one line, one thread of composing, recomposing, building the broken down, a bit now of an author's own two hands in it. *Text is tissue*, Roland Barthes tells us in his theory of its pleasure. Acker builds her own body up in words, inklings, strings it variably with weights and piercings. A girl is trying to learn to feel worth. In "Notes on the Life of Baudelaire," for $L=A=N=G=U=A=G=E$ magazine, she explains it as, "This is the only way I can act. This is the only way I can write. Bad." Handling fears through knowing her own recesses, a girl is creating nuance in experience. PORTRAIT: *...I can think and masturbate and write, which is the only activity this evil society has left me capable of doing.*

16.

The slip of Harold Robbins's text into her own Acker cues with the spoken command, "Look," picked up from the mouth of his conniving character Jacques, being employed in *The Pirate* to surreptitiously get compromising pictures of married, pleasure-cruising Jordana, a celebrity first lady now in Acker. Where Jacques and Jordana have been embroiled for over three months, the unnamed Acker stand-in for this man admits his motivation and tries to seduce with a line: "Three nights I've been following you." While some of Acker's re-purposing admittedly is even less mincing of words (Jacques releases "his erect penis from his bikini" or a *young dark-haired man* lets out a cock), she makes a combination of moves: heightening in the quoting, but also recasting: as a man on the street like a cocksure character straight out of a Harold Robbins novel approaches the narrator, acting herself in authoring some perverse mimeticism, as if she were the one and only, Jackie. The invitation to oral sex Robbins's Jordana dismisses in favor of a glass of white wine. Acker lets it hang, by cutting from entreaty to inside next a disco. "Papagayo" or "The Metropole" might be neither here nor there. "No one thought it strange that a woman or a man wanted to dance alone" in the south of France, likewise in the middle of New York City. Who cares if the man she's dancing with went to a French school or a New York private one? At times, dipping into Robbins's world pulls into Acker's own such rare-find materials for me as "mudders." *You look like a fast-track lady and there's nothing but mudders out there....* He lives just past "Le Gorille" for Robbins or "the Paradise" in Acker.

17.

I will mean the verb in a double-sense here, as I collapse career production into one word-fold I dutifully will as well unpack: Acker mines transgression in two moves. As fielded, Acker's "schizophrenia" was one of the rhetorical land mine: blown up to show words stable dependent on contextual surround, soundness. She dropped them in and around each other, swaths of shells echoing them wrecking the independent appearance of neighbors. Her *smoothe*r constructions, post-*Empire* (1988): create, rather than large-scale chaos, pulls in the line of the sentence and snags in continuance of the law, the psychoanalytic "name of the father" made real, as reeled through Acker characters and tropes: the father made Judge, Daddy boyfriend, or a negotiation afoot between the two, to engulf the straight linear logic, in Derrida's neologism *phallogocentrism* ("father/prick," she notes on a diary page in a series she was doing early called "The Creation"). AMERICA: *when I say fuck fuck means anything.* Opening one of her late compositional notebooks, this one for *Pussy, King of the Pirates*, Acker has copied inside a Cixous quote from which to begin training sights, dreaming...plotting. "There are two ways of clambering downward—by plunging into the earth and going into the sea—and neither are easy." With Cixous again on the cover of another archived notebook, "Paradise is down below." Still, we could see this as part of a reading as the tarantula feeds: entering into a corpus of another, penetrating with the fang-pen-finger, typing, or gliding *phallus*. That other body is set into a dissolve, as the tarantula begins to hold that destroyed mass together in the ball of silk it weaves around the other, then taking its nourishment from the sack. A final armor she dons of Eurydice is grounded in earth, archived there even.

18.

It is through Acker's work that I have become interested in and invested in fields of interpenetrating significance I enter into here. I do not, as you will see, primarily desire to isolate individual works of hers or her utterances. I see Acker's works on a continuum, and one not necessarily straightforward. There are as many roads to take as halls of mirrors to trip down potentially, words or cue cards, signs to interpret within and without of the given contexts, footing can be hard. That which "pricks" me there within her, a pricking often contingent upon my prior investments—even given these little puncta, to adapt from his formulation, Barthes himself would be one—I can see how I recourse to the narrative of Acker's career development, more often than not, in an initial desire to survey thoroughly. As Acker herself writes in "The Seattle Book": *Content is non-replaceable values (differences or words) in time.* Or as such conception is made metaphoric in "Lust," as her sailor laments: *Every one-night stand or man in a one-night stand is like every other one-night stand or man in a one-night stand because the sex in a one-night stand is without time and only time allows value.*

19.

In *My Death My Life by Pier Paolo Pasolini* (1984), that famed poet director's working-class cruises, and his subsequent vulnerability at the hands of the higher powers of politics, can still be seen to lead to his death. Still, even after being killed, the character of Pasolini in Acker will announce how he is going to begin working on solving his own murder. In Acker, there will be no simple means and ends. In her words, in his mind, this would be "by denying the principle of causation and by proposing nominalism." The reader looks up or turns the page. Pasolini doesn't return by name as we continue forward. Acker foregrounds intent—"this working a way of living"—and procedure—"the procedural point of view we want to privilege"—in the earlier work, *Rip-off Red, Girl Detective*. As a subjectivity already flexed toward the radical becomes finessed more highly and as it gains in sophistications, it goes the more undercover. To study Pasolini in the book she elects to name for him: an initial life episode, which begins the narrative, moves on shortly to an investigation of attendant desires and an extensive chalking out of some underlying societal structures by the author. In the case of Acker's "Pasolini," this is done primarily through a "deconstruction" of Shakespeare's plays (*in the American sense*, to use Lotringer's modification of one of her offerings in their interview), status quo schooling states if ever there were ones. In inserting her own acting-out autobiographically into that venerable bard's setups of history and romance, taking on the character lenses of traditional and canonical schooling, in re-fusing these bastions, Acker revels. What will she have to do, and to whom, to see her own self there lying? Another thing Acker wants to get to the bottom of is just what the self might be left at a liberty to dream, once regulatory identifications have taken place and then been reinforced.

20.

In Art, associations that have become automatic are those we should work to loosen and stretch, to trouble and expand. "Appropriate" are called those responses that have been trained in. They have entered through *normal*: acquisition of language and its usage under tutelage of what you can see in psychoanalysis called the Father's NO. This training is that entrance into Symbolic order: a weaning. It is learning a system of rewards, controls, learning there is time and a place for everything, when we begin to do as they all say. Words come in the place of cries, and you might begin to ask nicely. EXPECTATIONS: *Nightmare: her body mirrors/becomes her father's desire.* In his interview by Acker, Burroughs continues to emphasize the necessity of destroying what he calls "the word"—the restrictive construction, that where open-ended, and any generous overflow, with meaning, waysides.

21.

Writing becomes more how Acker develops aspects in individual sentences and sections of her work, accents against others, providing effects of the telescoping and refocusing. This is the *Pussy, King of the Pirates* attack plan of divided narrators, rounded up through a preface together, intercut with a letter Artaud is rewriting and re-writing to a third party George Le Breton, the document itself one that moves from a defense of poetry—from a kind of "against interpretation"

(SS) defense—to psychology, to hallucination, through which Acker situates a reading of Heidegger's Being in light of Hitler, which she inserts then into the letter, moving on to a third-person section ("In the Days of Dreaming"), intercut with large swathes of quotations from outside sources, often unanchored, to float there, to other "manuscripts," found, folded in, other addresses, etc. A line in a *poem* placed within the work of her *Great Expectations* book: *Fiction by my will will become the most / popular form.* In her speech for the Artist in Society Conference, of "a close friend of mine, a poet," Acker says she "desired to find her own structures, thus contents."

22.

It is arguable that a significant other also fulfills something akin to a diary function, as in *Empire of the Senseless* Acker situates the issuing forth of her text from a body even more theatrically there in a frame. An opening parenthetical to the book orients: Abhor *speaks* through Thivai, we read, before we are then told (read) "her" story: Acker's Abhor words reportedly coming from the source of Thivai. Bodies hold these stories, other than just their own stores. One set of arrangements screen another, as we read the words of one through another, and he keeps her history, contained, smothered, or safe. She sets them up as part of larger unfolding showcase, hers.

23.

Acker's postmodern takes on the genre of detective mysteries or fictions would be books that attempted to "solve" issues of body and its relation then to identity. The deaths can be literal or more metaphorical ones of bodies just too sexually alone, adrift. As she continues to grow, intellectually, as a writer, cutting prose-teeth more, and mind sharpening, her books then become increasingly complex in the valences of multi-rhetorical juggling that they undertake. As her public persona consolidated, over time, as she became more well-known, in her later books the construction of personality moved to sites more within her books' insides, away from its early situation in that legal, overt location of the authorial signature. IDENTITY: *Had decided I was going to act so I put on a disguise of a grey fedora, just like the one the judge used to wear* over the eyes (*Oedipus was blind*), and a too-long navy coat, like the ones the schoolgirls used to wear, *and black high-heeled shoes.* Original emphasis.

24.

"Until fairly recently, we had to be either prostitutes or wives. Therefore our very economic subsistence was absolutely dependent on our bodies, yet at the same time we weren't allowed to talk about this. It was OK for a man to use certain terms, and even today you read Henry Miller, James Joyce and no one says that those guys are pornographic, but for a woman to use those terms, suddenly you get pornography," she explains in an *Argonaut* newspaper interview. She also says: *Words which formerly applied to degraded ways of life now are used proudly and words once used with sacred delight are now forgotten.* This was to be one of the starting principles for her version of translation of Aristophanes, his "Ladies Day," or "celebrating ladies" as it could also appear in English. Ackerian premise: when criticizing, cultured tones would not cut it. In a draft of the planned essay to be titled "After the End of the Art World," she quotes from the beginning of the *Cyberfeminist Manifesto for the 21ˢᵗ Century*, "We are the modern cunt positive anti-reason unbounded unleashed unforgiving..." Where the respected Barthes had said in his *Pleasure* fragment "Politics" how "The text is (should be) that uninhibited person who shows his behind to the *Political Father*," Acker would show rather and we see her *cunt*—her word, choice to examine. PORTRAIT: *I open the red lips of my cunt and begin to laugh.* DON: *Swear by your cunt. Only your cunt is holy.* A drafting for Jeanne Duval, "Because my memories are hiding in these hairs, this night, in order to resurrect my memories & make them deathless, I'm going to wave your cunt hairs as if they're banners right now in front of the public's faces."

25.

In large measure, I began to pursue a doctoral degree as a reaction to not having a proposed paper accepted for the *Lust for Life* event, despite eventual lunches. I had begun in Georgia to read her about a year before she died, all the novels, and then the essays, in a rapid series finishing one, starting another, in a period of just a few months. As part of opening night *Lust for Life* presentations, Eve Kosofsky Sedgwick as a special guest read a thread through one book, the dreams in *My Mother: Demonology*. A second decisive factor for me to pursue another degree was in a letter exchange with Wayne Koestenbaum, in which I offered to him essays I was doing that he called in an encouraging response performative. One angled itself up against and through the Acker book of Colette Peignot, a.k.a. "Laure," and Georges Bataille, another *My Mother* aspect, a romance transposed not only to Acker's own dynamics from family, beyond blood, but in one chapter as well (four: "Obsession") that famed, psycho-sexual geography of Emily Brontë's *Wuthering Heights*.

26.

I regret that book of essays, culled from the *Lust for Life* event held just five years after Acker's death, does not contain three of the presentations I found particularly provocative and further generative for my own thinking. Liz Kotz's proposed reevaluation of Acker within a line of Cageian poetics. Caroline Bergvall took up "dog writing," as suggested by Acker's reanimating of Cervantes's Sancho Panza in a talking bitch. Susan E. Hawkins considered mourning and the maternal in Acker's late fiction and was working on this in relation to another difficult writer published to wider audiences: Cormac McCarthy, with his "cold war cowboys."

27.

In Memoriam to Identity, in a trail of gender-logic: *Since she hadn't had and obviously wasn't going to have a baby, must be a man. Or she had been born complete and instantaneous, she would have said, a hero.* It was almost two decades before that, in "The Burning Bombing of America," before ole Oed's name is specifically popping up often in her lexicon: "psychoanalysis? no. government? no. family? no." Once entrenched firmly in her period of myths, though, Acker begins to take Oedipus back in her making of this story of metaphors that grounds Freud and his inheritors' psychoanalysis just one more in a series of "classics" over which to engage. Acker begins to explore then why Orpheus would do just as well, and much more poetically. He by the way comes not with a mother but Eurydice in tow. The kingdoms at stake display difference in kinship to him.

28.

Acker would never be one of those women, "mothers," who place men before their own daughters, forsaking them. *In Memoriam to Identity*: the Father "had once given me fifty dollars when I had begged him for it and the next day my mother had instructed me that if I didn't instantaneously give it back to him and apologize to him, I'd have to leave their home forever." Acker would fight too what she perceived as simplifications in certain theorists. In *Some Other Frequency*: "Take Cixous's argument against Kristeva, with Cixous saying that our problems all have their source in genital difference— so that the fact that men have cocks is what makes them evil." "She's a separatist." To begin with, Acker philosophically triangulates Cixous with another woman. What she does is create a difference between two women, two poles. I notice as I myself am given to such configurations, as my method of working through Acker here will strongly attest I'm sure. This is due in large part to sexuality, my identification with her, through sexuality...chicken, egg. *Frequency*, again: "Kristeva's argument that the real problem has to do with role models makes a lot more sense to me." It is the way society is organized, not men in it, with which Acker has her primary problem. Emphasized there in the same interview: "*I like men.*" In that source too her laugh is noted around, "the milkman still has to deliver the milk." Her grievance with Cixous does not keep Acker from trying to work with her. It is part of the journey Acker is on in *Pussy, King of the Pirates*. The notations from Cixous's work on journals Acker composed sections and drafts of this novel in show this. She begins to take even someone like Cixous apart, to make *part-objects* of the theorizing, but she does not confine herself either to only one theory. She makes the spilling articulations of Cixous into one body that can be managed, parceled out satisfactorily within the ebb and flow of Acker's own fluctuating party lines. She fashions an array of the available measures around her, toys with them within their colors, sizing herself up, temperaments with which to pleasure texts.

29.

Our initial set of concerns in the *Toulouse* book, "The Case of the Murdered Twerp," "Longing for Better Things," "The Desperation of the Poor," and how the issues so far raised might all relate are moved—or abandoned—forward through Chapter Four, "The Creation of the World," for other stories of other conflicts more various in source it seems. Here is a fable, a biosphere of prose in gendered politics and evolutionary, colonizing concerns, and philosophical for all that, of a little cat so in love with a big baboon she will unwittingly help him, feeding him, to take over the world and to create a new order for it. PORTRAIT: "She'll do anything so the big hairy baboon'll love her." "She's starving." And: "Now the horrible baboon's stomach is so huge, it rubs against the white moon. The stomach is so dense, it weighs as much as the earth. So there exist three balls: earth, baboon, moon." The little cat set to dreaming of an Eden before the baboon where it is only once the "white bears rise up," once on hind legs there and, *bat their paws against each other's faces*, we have the first period in this passage. The sentence that proceeds after the period confirms the end of a dream. PORTRAIT: *This is how the world came to be.*

30.

Our next story now that *the world exists* brings war home as we read through the sap of a voice longing, frightened, and confused romantic, the story of harrowing near date-rape, then find further the cause of frigidity that offends to be rooted in an earlier rape by brother Ted: "just gotten back from Nam and he hadn't quite adjusted yet to our peaceful home." Sis is suited up in red silk pajamas, so he can give "what all of you yellow bitches want." During this dress-up scene of how house has been played overseas, he offers, "You can pretend you're a little Vietnamese girl." This then is the prince she gets.

31.

A final story to consider in a veritable mini-trilogy in itself, in Chapter Four, in *Toulouse*, is the one that would take up a Harold Robbins-like reader challenge to "guess who everyone is really supposed to be" in his book—and, if you like such language play, hijacks it, heightening it even, even while laying barer the foundation. Lotringer calls her method *terrorism in literature*, as pirating force Acker becomes, re-investing a narrative in Robbins's book into its obvious ends more openly, run it ashore. Here is a place to stress too that many of Acker's appropriations function through a desire to amplify, complicate, to further some previous benchmark. These may be the lows of Robbins or even some philosophical probe to be found in tales of Poe. In *I Dreamt I Was a Nymphomaniac*, "Peter's story" goes like this. In part, a trace of the *Nymphomaniac*'s primary given "I" misrecognizing its self in bits of "Peter," and then trying to make of Peter and his story a twin or double, Acker composes in large measure there from another story with which Peter's own structurally couples and echoes, Edgar Allan Poe's tale of unfortunate identity-split, "William Wilson." Dogging an original hounds a character back. Or there are parrots, with distortion. Acker's take on Robbins's *The Pirate* begins: *My name is Jacqueline Onassis...* Robbins's catalyzing bombshell in his setup is replaced in Acker's by the "classy," once epitome of glamorous insider, once commandeer-in-chief's woman, looking now for erasure, casting among the anonymous: *I was walking along the street. I wasn't doing anything. I was looking for some action.* To flaunt relative associations and values, Acker walks bestselling author downtown, to become willing punk. Acker details her text by redeploying the means in which the other has been decked out. Wanna slum? Sometimes it remains—like life— unclear at whose expense the joke is. She determines what to take rogue from Robbins and how to use it in fun and games or not so innocently. Both versions of this mirroring scene of pleasure-seeking have a character cautioning the amour picked up to "keep things in their proper perspective," be that the accompanying cock play on open seas rather than the beach or a darker bar than in public in the street. Acker puts it through re-staged paces, loads it up, nudging and shifting grounds for its containment, taking his notes in a kind of regurgitation, in recitation. When the Robbins vehicle feels "the wetness between her legs," *I* feel it between *my legs* and his bisexual Jacques further bases a now similarly pre-disposed "Jackie"/ Acker. She shares the sex it must be me? Jordana is conveyed by: *the seventy-thousand dollar San Marco.* The Robbins intrigue takes place in the environs of Cannes. Acker's "Jackie" takes to the city bright sidewalk for prospective invites. (This is what is proclaimed "the true story of a rich woman.") Acker transposes to a New York *resort* of Times Square. *The neon lights were blinking at me, winking, inviting hot desires I had never known existed.* And: *I began to move with him.* The way the prospective dances allows Onassis protagonist to decide, "You're from the South, aren't you?" Like me. In that book my "mixed," fundamentalist, Southern nieces and nephews are not bound to be reading anytime soon: *"Cracker country," he said. "Georgia."*

32.

To make her way, her own legend had it, Acker worked for a time in a sex show in Times Square, and in dire straits, many of Acker's characters will have to resort to some version of the occupation. PORTRAIT: *My friends were all respectable (i.e. had minimum money): I couldn't ask them shit. So I opened the back pages of the* Village Voice. *In less than three hours I became a go-go dancer.* And: *I figured I could sell my body, a resource open to most young women, not for a lot of money but at least for more than eighty dollars a week and less than eight hours a day.* That sentence was issued in the seventies. Writing my dissertation, 2/21/07: *Village Voice* back pages I quickly peruse still promisingly enticed and competitively, when you considered inflation: "in need of girls who want to make $1000/day"; "$500 a day at least"; "Are you a Black or Hispanic woman with way too many bills?" Quoting verbatim a newspaper advertisement, why is race marked here? The times they are not a-changin', though inflating, keeping pace conflating. *I Dreamt I Was a Nymphomaniac*: "I was rolling my ass around in the lousy bar on Folsom Street the Folsom Street Bar where they hold slave-auctions...." PORTRAIT: "A go-go dancer is a strip-tease artist, midway in the hierarchy between a high-class call girl and a streetwalker." Docile, doll-toy, I object to drive and move around the floor, field, as seen fit she's to have no mind. Markets shift through social issues. DON: "I lived on the outskirts of, in the lowest part of, society because I worked a sex show; then I believed that I deserved to be shat on, that if I didn't pull myself up by non-existent bootstraps out of the muck I would die, and that I had to be very tough."

33.

Even before its actual working, the power of the strip scene, dynamics of control, is shown to be present in a couple of childhood humiliations in *Rip-off Red, Girl Detective*. First, the hands of a grandmother go to proudly show off just how mature the narrator is getting. Here it begins for a young girl on her eighth birthday, taken to The Hotel Grift for her party: *my grandmother lifts up my pink dress to show the headwaiter my new girdle. New York lechers. I hate this part of my life.* It is one with pink flowers sewn on it that her mother has "stuck" her into. Next comes initiatory dare, the grounds for becoming part of the childhood club-gang our heroine has established with some others, shortly thereafter: "only by completely stripping in front of us on a rainy day in Central Park." As the option for gainful employment, it is moved already through as part of our opening, character profile, getting the ball rolling: "I'm five foot three inches brown hair curling all over my face, bright green eyes, I'm 26 but my body's tough from dancing if you know what I mean— well I got bored doing a strip, well first, I got bored doing that Ph.D. shit and being frustrated professors' straight-A pet, especially being faithful to a husband who spent all his time in bed dealing out poker hands; I left school, descended to the more interesting depths and became a stripper, even that finally bored me, so I decided, on my 26th birthday, to become the toughest detective alive." I compare this husband position above to in "Requiem" one of the mother figure's favorite pastimes seen, "*CLAIRE and the girl sit themelves on the former's bed. It is here that most of the life in this family happens. / CLAIRE reaches for the deck of cards that's always on her bedside table and shuffles them pro-style.*"

34.

In *The Adult Life of Toulouse Lautrec by Henri Toulouse Lautrec*, the whorehouse is cut back to, a whorehouse we are reminded of never actually having left no matter how caught up in the preceding fantasy of the woman called Jackie O. we might have become in floating through Robbins as stage designed by Acker. Acker's metaphor for reality here in this work, and one that colored many others, is to be stuck in the whorehouse. The novelty of the new story would only be good for so long, before once again reality rudely intrudes. ADULT: '*O, cut the shit,*' *Norvins says, dragging her huge body into the room.* The entering character is one running "the hottest bar in

Montmartre. In the back of the bar's a whorehouse." Whores, fantasy facilitators and for-hire fulfillers, have been telling each other bedtime stories all along, it seems, and this latest in a string is the one featuring the fallen president's wife. The author lies in wait, another narrative trick, while we have been following, trying to, guilelessly, to fit some dream pleasantly. Like way back then, as Emily Brontë found it a solution to do, when the storied romance needed more expanse, she laid another generation down upon foundations of the first, Acker in *The Adult Life* follows suit with further future relations. More time is needed. Without the trek becoming too loose, meet now "Marcia, young daughter of Vincent Van Gogh," who has taken up with a character only identified at first by another profession: "the architect."

35.

Here I am concerned with the framing of fictions, her positioning and repositioning, theoretically, and a milieu I think of as compatriots, receptive or not so to accomplishments to be and opened up through her.

36.

Journeying would be a looser mechanism of plotting along. Journeying is how Acker makes her identities: she strings narratives along a setting out—progressing in the time books might provide. The cat. The homo I am on a prowl. The eye of every word on the way open: wandering sailor, visionary masturbator or plundering pirate, the poet arriving at and seeking climax defined running a steak all through it.

IDENTITY: "R sat in his mother's house and masturbated. He no longer wanted to go anywhere but masturbating." A directive is doled out to that bastard—get out of the house. PORTRAIT: *My parents kicked me out of the house because I wasn't interested in marrying a rich man....* It's what you do when you must go seek your fortunes, elsewhere. Even the ol' standard bearer of psychoanalysis, Oedipus, is too shown through it eventually how he doesn't know just what he thought he did, didn't know enough, really, or now knew too much to be proceeding along that same track as he was traveling before. Once that O gets all filled up, once meaning of his dreaming is revealed to him, tilled, the truth of what Cixous coins "the little circus" seen... I would like to shift now to that ungendered pronoun, one. I won't stick to the masculine, even for the sake of "clarity." These are her works: symbolic economy ruptures. One feels one must repress what one has seen. One goes to pieces, turning knowledge in upon one's self. Acker, too, desires to investigate other enterprising routes than simply getting better. Successfully navigating or coming through her Oedipus complex, to put it less lyrically, in more clinically recognizable terms; such recovery pegs her, has her acknowledge one leg—she simply supports through a fundamental absence, alack—some grander scheme.

37.

The fact that many of the theorists that Acker questions or outright lampoons she calls upon in interviews to help her to discuss her own aims in writing must be accounted for. One in particular is Deleuze, seen among a motley crew in *Don Quixote*, though she also seems to quote him in all earnestness as an authority in the essay "Good and Evil in the Work of Nayland Blake." The aims are not static, and thus how appropriate or serving she finds any thinker at any given moment to or for her own philosophical ends rightly illustrates a fluctuation in valuation. None are to be set in stone. As she is watching it be made before her very eyes, Acker documents the cultural history. In a document like this one, I do simultaneously perpetuate and fetishize the cachet of an increasingly dated milieu. I do it because these sources have at times attracted me also, though this is a fantasy often easier to maintain if one has not met the individual reference in question in actual person. By 1993, Acker becomes more reticent seemingly about "proper" identities in the pages of *My Mother: Demonology* than she had shown herself to be in the past. Despite this fact, particular characters leak through in the interventions of interviews. To take Lotringer again, ever present to link, it is only a few steps from an admission with him in "Devoured by Myths," "Well, meeting you changed me a lot..." to a couple of years on in the fiction of *My Mother*, "My ex-boyfriend on the tour, a theorist, journalist, and fiction writer, explained that he had brought postmodernism into the United States." This is some math that a kid like me could feel some satisfaction accomplishing.

38.

In "The Path of Abjection," McCaffery asks, "Why inhabit other texts rather than starting out with something of your own?" She replies how, "The honest answer has to do with my personality, even with my sexuality. Kristeva's *Powers of Horror* opened up this area for me so that I could understand certain aspects about myself and my creative process." And, goes on. "What I also recognize now is that I am passive. Deeply, deeply passive. So the quality of making or creation that comes out in me—whatever it is in me that has to do with making—is based on a reactive rather than an active principle. I don't see a blank page when I'm writing. Ever. Or when I do, nothing happens."

39.

She divides her career in the Lotringer interview into movements of, roughly, the "conceptual," the "nihilist" (American deconstructions) and the making of new myths, narratives. It is in this last period that Acker decides to begin to try to work past experiment as the end in itself, just one compositional mode, that she began to cite openly a number of poststructuralist female theorists, though it is as early as in one of her notebooks for the Jeanne Duval work that she can be seen noting: "Jouissance adds/joins force to desire." The "Oedipal-obsessive" critics a character in one book rants against are aired by Acker in other realms of culture when she is trying to explain, place among them, her own brand of artistic productions. She would be a poet-novelist that sees herself in a context of philosopher writers. The apparent favorite, Kristeva, might not be said to exhibit in her more academic treatises such an obvious concern with making the surface writerly in transporting apothegms as bite-sized, late Barthes, or the veiled drifting of Cixous in her escapes, the brilliantly wrung opaqueness that crystalizes Irigaray, but even Kristeva succumbs in a sideline to aesthetic practice: that vocabulary ramped down a notch or two, relaxing points driven home in the detective fictions she has penned.

40.

The subject of theory becomes part of the drama in Acker's piece, "Russian Constructivism," appearing in *Blasted Allegories*. This anthology of "writings by contemporary artists" presents work by Laurie Anderson, Theresa Hak Kyung Cha, Sherrie Levine, Jenny Holzer (including her truism "A NAME MEANS A LOT JUST BY ITSELF"), and Richard Prince (the subject of another of Acker's essays, "Red Wings"). *Blasted Allegories* credits "Russian Constructivism" as a reprint from *Don Quixote*, where it appears labeled TEXT 1 in, "The Second Part of Don Quixote: Other Texts." I will attempt to give a sense of how this piece moves, some of the territory it covers, be that as fiction, or printed as essay (as it is included also in Acker's *Bodies of Work* collection), or art writing in and of itself. One line when this writing is within the novel is elsewhere absent: *Is there such a thing here as true love: that violence that's absolutely right?* The "here," ostensibly, is St. Petersburg. Then we are told how, "St. Petersburg is actually the Nevsky Prospect," before St. Petersburg is eventually shortened to: *in Peter*. Discrepancies in paragraphing between the various publications may be just house style. A touch of concrete poetry is made out of visual representation of a section of "newspaper below her fallen body," that body belonging to a female weightlifter. Eight interrupted lines of the paper run from both the left and right sides of the page, towards a center margin, to illustrate demarcating of two columns of newspaper, and what we are essentially given is a negative, an outlined area filled in by words hedging in representing what is hidden, in the jurisdiction of the body that has narratively fallen, creating shape on the page of its regulated ink fields. A dot matrix pattern makes a grayer background, further simulating the newspaper clipping, in one printing, absent in the others, all headed across the board with a title: CITY OF PASSION. *Please understand me. Please believe what's in my mind at this very moment. I do everything you want*, making up part of the piece, is one letter to Peter. In the middle of another, a Shakespeare appropriation is cut to through a parenthetical stage direction *(My nurse enters and binds me up)* interrupting that missive's progress. Justification differences between the book and standalone rendering exist. "The Poems of a City" (ON TIME, WILL VERSUS CHANCE, TIME IS IDENTITY, LONELINESS, TIME IS PAIN, TIME IS MADE BY HUMANS) are part 2 of the piece. The first poem's title is rendered smaller in the essay book, more like a subtitle to part 2. And then there is another source of variance, before the passage that I most want to point to, one to question the worthwhileness of attention to such details I have just practiced, the slightly differing of words in venue. With this I will go further. In part 5 ("Deep Female Sexuality: Marriage Or Time"): in the novel, "I'm only interested in abstract thought." A "my" found inserted in *Blasted Allegories* carries over to the reprinting that presents the piece later as essay, to read: *I'm only interested in my abstract thought.*

41.

'I know you know a good many of my New York friends and I've always wanted to talk with you about your work': begins a dialogue exchange between unattributed speakers. The next paragraph prompts, "What did we talk about?" Further setting out of this conversational exchange, speakers still unattributed, and this time for twenty lines, ~36 sentences, fragments of sentences dropped in and moved out of among

more complete ones, to include one curious instance of lacuna, where a line gives over to much silent white space only…before the words starting back up within a quoted space we are still within, it seems, to question whether or not the present party, gender of both speakers throughout the passage unmarked in any way, believes there is something *fishy* in certain semiotic theories. Pointed to especially are Deleuze and Guattari. Answer? "There's a gap now…" After this point, the use of ellipses begins to imply guesses, or hazarding, trailing off, in particular around any absolutes…before someone it appears picks up a book, and a quick, certain exchange on the subject ends in the next sentence stopping for the reader the dialogue, "Kiss." *We don't stop kissing each other now.* Somewhere in the midst of all the talk that could be classed academic: "I remember in New York when semiotics came only it was Sylvère who brought it over, what it really did was give me a language with which I could speak about my work. Before that I had no way of discussing what I did, of course I did it, and my friends who were doing similar work we had no way of talking to each other." They make friends. There in *My Mother: Demonology*, an ex-boyfriend is *'a kind of cultural emissary.'* Importing theory, "his only purpose had been to annoy and so, to wake up, the American left-wing academic establishment. For both he and the French theorists had understood, and understand, that postmodernism, all that theory, is a joke. To his amusement, the Americans had completely misunderstood postmodernism and turned it into an academic discourse." It is a joke Acker wants to be in on. It is a joke too I run the risk of falling prey to, making too many high-minded claims ever for her work. I could recall how above here we are in a supposed work of "fiction" (essay in the guise of fiction? pointed story), a game we might often be hard-pressed to remember how we are playing, as many of the sentences, setups and situations reverberate, and fit together, and when we find ourselves in some moments of her prose creating another version of a story she has told somewhere elsewhere before. These tendentious couplings her work often does everything to fortify. Periods of historical assertion in the prose contribute to and allow arguably for her work to succeed in its gravitation between genres. A fictional episode easily becomes the basis for some art writing if containing the right kinds of characters, names, essaying, or testing out, some knowledge of them.

42.

It is not only through Freud and his theories, obviously, the father, as Acker would site it, could also find his place, to root around within artistic lineage—those male—even those of the more avant-garde stripes. To recourse, Acker would attempt to subsume—Freud-Oedipus—all the other hims/ *hymns* she comes across on her way, a plethora, threading. She attempts then to trace queerer lines than a solely Oedipal drama of identity construction, at the same time that she tries to work—consciously—in the face of him, "Oedipus." O is a sign that includes and swallows, engulfs, takes that puss down into its hole, whole engulfing self. AMERICA: *can't remain in enemy territory*. If they don't treat her and respond to her as she would like, she would incorporate, take their worded bodies into her own, their output packed up for further travels, another artistic family dusted. Acker riffs in making Oedipus into just another story-poem, cum with Freud and Dora of whom H. Cixous in *La Jeune Née* says: "I read it like fiction." What Acker emphasizes, when she does and if she must take as a starting point Oedipus, is the orphan status. To begin with he is by his parents abandoned out into a desert where he was to be seen from never again. The last thing they expected was he would not be killed. The last thing they expected was for him to find a way back eventually home.

43.

A poem in both Farsi and English translated is part of the makeup of *My Mother: Demonology*. Not surprisingly perhaps, *In Memoriam to Identity*, revolving largely around a retelling of sexual dynamics between Rimbaud and Verlaine, also contains poems: one called "To The Germans Both Nazis And Peaceniks" attributed to Baudelaire. One "R," and hear here the pirate, too, *arrgh*, Rimbaud "copped from Baudelaire." As Rimbaud can be said to descend from Baudelaire—Rimbaud consciously positions himself in one of his letters an heir, calling Baudelaire "first among seers, the king of Poets, *a true God*," complaining "yet he lived in too aestheticized a world," declaring "the inventions of the unknown demand new forms"—Acker has herself precedents for her own ante-upping in the Rimbaud example. Not quite doing her "copying," Rimbaud does get his feel from elsewhere, a sense of what could be entered, further expanded and expounded upon, and as in Acker, his life and work through and through are married. Lines of a poem start a chapter, *In Memoriam to Identity*: "Idle youth enslaved to everything / let the time come when hearts feel love," or the "I" dress up as pirate in the *aye*.

44.

The transgression might be made metaphoric in the symbolic "cannibalizing"—girl's got to eat—of the forefathers' words, the mind ingesting, a gesture, gestation, jestering of the consuming, sleep with the mother she would never let herself become, or only for herself, in her art, as Acker tries to take down all of the larger than life powers, to not let them be. Acker plays with their ideals as bodied ideas, so many accoutrements, like so many manageable objects. In enlarging: what's been kept from her becomes somewhat internalized if knowable. To be more inside her own body, she worked to create a rift between herself and a 19th-century, Victorian, realist view of the novel. This is cut through in reliance upon a privileging of poetic languages. These could be seen to be capitalist-patriarchal-order-revolting, as proposed through articulations of Kristeva. *Revolt, She Said*: "revolt, as I understand it—psychic revolt, analytic revolt, artistic revolt—refers to a state of permanent questioning, of transformation, change, an endless probing of appearances," "to think is to revolt, to be in the movement of meaning," "perennial interrogation-as-revolt." Also, Kristeva reminds us: *The word revolt comes from a Sanskrit root that means to discover, to open... A chest too.*

45.

In *The Adult Life of Toulouse Lautrec*, Acker sketches out the crime scene of the bordello there in a line drawing of the floor plan of the place: in one room, dining room, the dead body. Other rooms, though, are left identified with only question marks, shifting entrances and hidden thresholds *undiscovered*. This is true as well of one architectural draft of *Rip-off*

Red. There are other pictorial elements, too: "signs" quite graphically marked as such, words laid out on the page, set-off and boxed in like little routes to the book themselves: calling-card drawings, ads for services, and of notices—WOMAN AND CHILDREN ARE ALLOWED IN THIS BAR ONLY IF THEY ARE SILENT—mockups of newspaper headlines. On other maps the rooms may be left by no longer existing in time, typographical keys supplementing drawing designs explain. Traditional notions of time are folded in upon themselves, in masturbating, or "dreaming." A MAP OF TIME AND NO TIME in *My Mother* transforms a "central room among many rooms" through journeying out along a new perspective line to become then a *bag within bag*. I will leave you the unpacking of the word as such, said.

46.

What is this lack? This absence that drives me, Acker writes in working on a piece of "Jeanne Duval." A constant questioning, the questing, disrupts the safely defined position from within which one might locate comfortably an ego, self: "self," that costume we find mostly easily composed through an expense of some Other. Baudelaire, waxing poetic about the love object, through Acker's hand in her drafting the muse, "Aren't you the space in which I can begin to dream? Aren't you always wet inside? Aren't you the nipple out of which I suck memories' liquids?" To be striding more a poststructuralist, in later work like *My Mother: Demonology*, I would argue, mining the likes of Lacan, in: *All children come red out of the womb because their mothers know God*. All children come read. In that *Mother* book, the rewriter of Freud

167

appears in a sort of parenthetical confirmation: "According to Elisabeth Roudinesco in her study of Lacan, around 1924 a conjuncture of early Feminism, a new wave of Freudianism, and Surrealism gave rise to a new representation of the female: nocturnal, dangerous, fragile, and powerful. The rebellious, criminal, insane, or gay woman is no longer perceived as a slave to her symptoms. Instead, 'in the negative idealization of crime [she] discovers the means to struggle against a society [that disgusts]." The brackets Acker supplies. To see her work clearly, we must understand how it works itself out to be "other" than previous interpretations of Woman, *Other*, around her. RED: *his middle finger slips into my ass: that's the center of my brain! That's where all my thoughts are located!* She entered herself into a relationship with other prior meanings. Fathers would be fought challenging their formal, prized positions. IDENTITY: "Father was a dildo and a hanger-on." The essentialist mother-function comes for her under this jurisdiction. Desecration will be through inversions, gladly. There were to be no apologias for the living in and out of those experiences lopped off as sub-human. "V also told Mme. V that he and R have animal sex," is how the cop report filed by the *parents* goes, *In Memoriam to Identity*. No apologies either for those orientations called *wrong*. She holds them up. In the archived piece titled "Arthur Rimbaud Was Homosexual": *Above all Arthur Rimbaud hated hypocrisy, the deadness of the provincial bourgeois society into which he had been born. He wanted to go to a world that was pagan, a world in which politics sexuality language sensation and identity are interconnected.*

47.

The Tarot could help map directions, within the stability of its shifts, in which a plot might further evolve in Acker's books. MOTHER: *I asked the witch to tell me what was happening.* The reader is presented with a graphic, a spatial representation of the spread of the cards, interpretative jurisdictions, and indications of which ones have been dealt out from the deck. *Empire of the Senseless*, with its character half-human, half-robot, literalizing Acker's pet metaphor of the only way to live under capitalism without a problem: like a machine: *I threw a pack of Tarot cards to find out whether or not I should kill myself or not.* A scatter diagram follows this declaration. Starting towards the bottom of the page, an arrow along a vertical axis proceeds up from a point marked "time" before being brought into relation with a columned caption, formatted line-breaks creating, in description and emphasis:

(line of
influences
from past
through present
to future)

Inside the parentheses these are held. The bit of previous legend joins to a preceding arrow via dots making a diagonal pointer. If what all *time* might mean does not yet seem complicated enough, the center of the time-line holds the name of the book's love interest—*Abhor*—missing now in the narrative leading up to this page. It bisects: "My irrational self," a labeled horizontal axis. Another line dotted out to the left-hand corner further elucidates this *irrational self*, an aside parenthetically expressed: "(the present or / the central / question)." There are technically two tips to the vertical line arrowed from *time* through "Ab-hor" that arrives at a destination of a coordinate labeled:

> *Alexander the Great*
> *looks out over the*
> *world he's conquered.*

"My irrational self" lies horizontally in line with a left-hand point keyed "Art," glossed: *(line of / events / writing / from past / to present / to future).* "My irrational self" also importantly darts towards an area on the right-hand side marked "a happy home," a vector that is further complicated by a vertical column of text extending alongside, off to the right of it, up against the book's margin, travelling the length of most of that surface area. There, from bottom to top, reads: *self: / happy and lonely // environment:* with the last colon opening particularly onto nothing—or rather taking in all of the above territory, surround, and or also: the "self" situated under it in another column, further mapping, that indexes that "environment":

> *desire:*
> *to use myself*
> *as well as*
> *possible.*

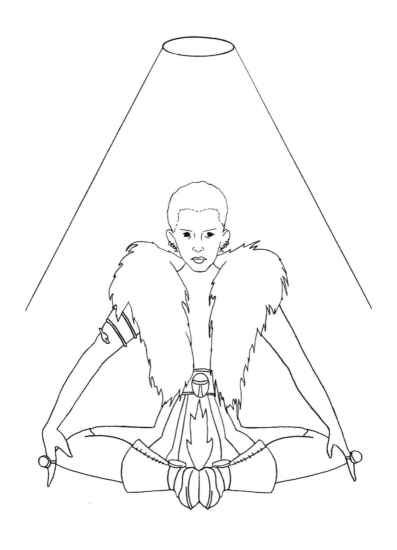

48.

illustration: Queen of Lights (Acker/Colette), Outsider Tarot
by Bobby Abate

49.

Coming out of the fields of complications in *Empire of the Senseless*, a tag of "conclusion: / death" might also be the overriding of the desire. Back to the tossed deck stacked. "These cards clearly showed that I liked the messed-up world in which I was living and that I was going to die. But it still wasn't clear, at least to me, whether I should kill myself or not." Kraus relates in her diary-keeping essay how Acker also records in her notebook she has a Tarot reading among other writings. In Acker's *Great Expectations*, the narrator, as her Tarot, called "a psychic map of the present, therefore: the future," is being read, claims April 18 her significator. Acker's protagonist Janey uses a Tarot deck in *Blood and Guts* with her father, Johnny: *Johnny's fortune is that he's gone through a bad time; now everything is clearing up; in the future a close friendship/marriage? With a woman; final result; a golden life.* This reading is ironically inflected, as we know Janey wants to be the one to stay with her father, happy. This convening of the two then gives onto a second, further shaping space for narrative, the dream. In a plethora of the definitions, every major Acker work negotiates them, as will many of her more minor pieces. "The Killers": *I didn't remember anything about this first period of my life, about my childhood. After this not remembering, I remembered jewels. As soon as my mother passed away, a jewel case was opened. The case, consisting of one tray, had insides of red velvet. Perhaps I'm dreaming my mother's cunt.* If the Tarot could provide a sort of foreshadowing, fanned watchwords, dreams provide alternate through clues reality. Dreams similarly might be interpreted as predictors, as the images shuffle out of the unconscious folds. As in a dream, in the writing she can watch herself. Pages in the book, card arrangements, augur or prompt paths. Even as she is doing it, she can see what she is doing. To Rickels: *I would leave the dream alone and use it to interpret the text.* She can begin to conceive of it as she begins to handle it. Such attenuates the anxiety, the psychoanalyst Melanie Klein tells in her pioneering modifications of techniques and theories that came before, adding to Freud's endeavors child play, her own analysis of language formation in symbolic grasp. Making more of them both, Acker rather tells her dreams to writing. The woman or girl in Acker is always trying to find a way, her way out, through her dreams.

50.

She does not know her father for real or even who he is, though later she would gather some suspicion. As part of a talk on narrative, published as "The Killers," she matter-of-factly presents the discovery. "When I was 26 years old, through an accident, I traced my father's family." This accident is not elaborated on there. She writes a letter to the man she believes may be him, a man she says she doesn't believe has ever met her, but she will explain as best she can. Chris Kraus writes to me after rereading my work. *Laura Jaramillo checked the Duke archives, but her scans don't include the letter K sent to her putative father....* Luckily I made a photocopy. The correspondence is dated from 1976. The way she came to the knowledge is bound up with a trust from her grandmother made out to Karen Lehman. Then an uncle told Acker how her father's parents came from Buffalo and about a business they owned (one to do with hair). "To make a long detective story short," she chase cuts with her father. As I was writing my dissertation, I imagined the letter would be widely quoted by others in future studies of Acker and her work. Still I wanted to excerpt at length, to keep with some particularities of her voice: *I have always wondered who my father is. My mother and her mother refused to tell me who he is or what his name is.* A paragraph goes, "Since I've never really had a father, I have no idea what relations between fathers and their children are supposed to be—if that matters at all. I would like to meet you. However I have no wish to impose on you; I can understand if you would rather have nothing to do with me. By the way—I'm sure it doesn't matter—my desire to meet you has nothing to do with my mother or her side of the family; actually, we're not very friendly. Just for myself. I'm curious who you are, what you're like. I've been so for a long time." PS: "Even if you don't wish to see me, any information you could give me about yourself and, if possible, though recalling the past can be a nuisance, about your marriage with my mother etc. would be more than welcome."

51.

Dating from 1974, "Born For Trouble" looks to me to be one of the poems Acker never wanted to write, beginning:

> *I never knew my father*
> *I guess I didn't have one*
> *When my mom was three months pregnant*
> *The shit she lived with left her.*
>
> *Cause the man she loved left her*
> *My mom couldn't stand me*

When she couldn't ignore me
She'd tell me I'm nothing.

So I love men
More than any of them knows
Each time I fuck one
I give him my soul.

It goes on, lyric or poem. It is corroborated in biography by "The Killers" talk Acker gave for a panel called "In Extremis, Writing at the Century's End" (April 29, 1993). "I have to tell you a few details about my childhood and about before my childhood.... I never met my father. Though he was married to my mother, he left her when she was three months pregnant with me." Her issue becomes narration, so Acker tells a story. In it she tells how she is given the idea that her real father might be an actual murderer. Then, in one succinct sentence: *When I was 30 years old, my mother suicided.* A finer point is put upon it all with her next sentence, "Enough of my childhood." Childhood, by the implication of narrative, lasts until the point of a mother's death.

52.

IDENTITY: *Cats who haven't been nursed properly all their lives claw and I...* PORTRAIT: *After stroking me, so I feel like a cat...* AMERICA: *leopards prowl between my legs.* As much as she identifies with the cats, big and small, animals to be worshipped, respected, honored just as much as the human, an other that may be a genderless preserve, the cat loved and fed again no matter how many times that wanders away from home, no matter how far, Acker identifies with Colette. Kristeva's "female genius work," the topic as well of a seminar that I sat in on, is divided into organization around three galvanizing figures, a trilogy of Colette with words, Melanie Klein around madness, and Hannah Arendt in the action of living the life. Colette was a woman too who once did not write under her own name. *Great Expectations* features pages from her book *The Pure and the Impure*, copied, clipped, reworded here and there, and these reworked pages would also be part of Acker's *The Birth of a Poet* play, copyrighted a year earlier than the *Great Expectations* novel. A few years later, Acker dates a Colette essay. "Being multiple her natural movement is to go outward, to roam," Acker explains in that essay, a work divided into four explanatory fields for playing Acker herself to tramp in while gathering significance. Prince, The Artist Formerly Known As, from 1993 to 2000, and now again, whom Acker writes of in *Don Quixote* under a text heading of "INSERT," is who should be elected President: on grounds similar to those she celebrates in Colette. *When he was thirteen, which is a magic number, he ran away from home just like Huckleberry Finn. He had nowhere to run to, cause there's nowhere to run anymore....* My ellipses. And as much as there is gender nonconformity in Colette as well, Acker sees in Colette a new myth, *European.* "Deconstruction is always a reactive thing and as long as you're dwelling in the reactive you're really reinforcing the society you hate." By the time that she is talking to Lotringer for "Devoured by Myths," Acker has begun working apparently on *My Mother: Demonology.* "So I got very interested with narrative. I started reading a lot of myths. I'm a Westerner with Greek myths..." The "European" myth, or Colette, as I read it might be opposed to Acker's view of one American. "In the United States, we're still living under the banner of the cowboy: that myth has led us to a supra-individualism, nationalism, and group paranoia," a quote from "After the End of the Art World," a part of her papers. In the Prince INSERT: *Prince believes in feelings, fucking, and fame…he'll be thirty years old when he gets elected President of the United States. Thirty years old is the height of male cowboy American rock 'n roll energy….* This is one of the things Acker sees the artist Richard Prince's work responding to admirably subverting: "When I see one of Prince's cowboys, I remember desire (my eyes on my father's cock), absence (daddy doesn't exist for me), and all the other feelings, contradictions, which show radical otherness or difference to me." (The other Prince, musician, who writes *SLAVE* on his cheek with the entertainment company and not he owning his recording masters, who changes his name to a symbol, is read "all-American because he's part black part white which is part good part evil." No part is purely one or the other, here, for her speaker.) The Colette myth formulates itself and functions as an escape through what is called sexuality, a sexuality outside of a decrying in *Blood and Guts in High School* that, "Sex in America is S & M." Rather than one that for her, or some of her characters is about "the glorification of slavery and prison," this sexuality here meets up with Acker's romantic fashioning and reliance upon a "pirate," sailor figure, the sailor of the slight identity ("Lust"), a myth of sexuality, as pluralizing, as that by which to live, a myth that might escape restrictive discourses of marriage and family as organized under one protective head, honcho. *According to Jesus Christ Our Lord, you too can become head (HE) of a multi-national corporation if you, following the teachings of Jesus Christ, give up enough and stop giving head (HE)*, the knight in *Don Quixote* can now declare, now that she is not afraid of anyone anymore. An untitled, incomplete manuscript in Acker's Papers: "If I couldn't marry well, I should be a doctor. If I had to be a writer, I should make lots of money. But that I, of my own free will, had chosen to live among the lowest of the low, pimps and strippers on forty-second street, and wrote unmentionable things in language which one couldn't quite name, neither prose nor poetry, neither experimental nor commercial, no law-abiding citizen could forgive much less understand this."

53.

In *Rip-off Red*, "Narratives you know are purely for shit. Here's the information go fuck yourself." Acker finds herself eventually banned in Germany, *Blood and Guts in High School*, or, as the German title would translate: *Tough Girls Don't Cry*. Banned with it in South Africa. She is banned in Canada with *Empire of the Senseless*. With Harold Robbins, she gets involved in legal problems. The charge in his case with her is plagiarism, how she put Jackie O. down into those pages where Robbins's trade had been a character "more Arab than Jew," to quote *The Pirate*, Robbins. To Lotringer, Acker disputes the validity of such gripes: "I have been very clear that I use other people's material." "I've always talked about it as a literary theory and as a literary method. I haven't certainly hidden anything." "So it's quite clear, I took the Harold Robbins and represented it." "Obviously appropriation has been some sort of postmodern technique in the arts for a number of years, both in the visual arts and the literary arts...." A public apology is demanded, one to which Acker ultimately must cave. This public story, though, and its implications are then source material for "Humility," collected in the anthology *The Seven Cardinal Virtues*, and then reworked in part to conclude *In Memoriam to Identity*. "Harold Robbins' publisher phoned up the man who ran the company who owned the feminist publishing company." IDENTITY: "Feminist publisher replied that she knew writer was actually a sweet nice girl." And: "CAPITOL MADE A DOLL WHO LOOKED EXACTLY LIKE HERSELF. IF YOU PRESSED A BUTTON ONE OF THE DOLL'S CUNT LIPS THE DOLL SAID, 'I AM A GOOD LITTLE GIRL AND DO EXACTLY AS I AM TOLD TO DO.'" And: "...sent a letter to the feminist publisher in which said that she composed her texts out of 'real' conversations, anything written down, other texts, somewhat in the ways the Cubists had worked." In a shade of the pedant, Acker pulls in a following bracket: *Not quite true. But thought this statement understandable.* (In "Russian Constructivism," asks: "Why's a Cubist painting, if it is, better art than a Vivienne Westwood dress?" It was during a residency at New Langton Arts that Dodie Bellamy first displayed some of Kathy Acker's clothes, "wheedled" in Bellamy's words from Matias Viegener. *Possessing such intimate effects of a woman I wasn't so much friends with as in awe of, I felt compelled to write it all out.*) In *The Seven Cardinal Virtues*, "Humility": WHAT IS IT? CAPITOL WROTE, 'TO BE AN ARTIST? WHERE IS THE VALUE THAT WILL KEEP THIS LIFE IN HELL GOING?

54.

Journeys take place in the mind, through the mirrors in the books. Our going from front to back can be one learned, but no matter how queerly we might choose to attempt a navigation, what we come to consider the reading experience is a time frame of some concentration, held to a degree. Knowing begins then may break off from what at hand is being held. Knowing can then try going off somewhere else. Journeying is a prime means of constituting narrative business. Movement to San Francisco would figure prominently in all of the works collected in *Portrait of an Eye*. In *The Childlike Life of the Black Tarantula*, the third part opens with a frame of "i move to san francisco." The fourth division of *I Dreamt I Was a Nymphomaniac: Imagining*, titled "san francisco and..." is where we read a deck stacked as, "Either I could get a new apartment in New York City or split to California, the only other place I had friends." Even before, in work unpublished but still bound by her, Acker is writing how: *I press my finger against my clit [ ] make plans to get to San Francisco [ ] no place to stay [ ] desire to move. [ ] end.* The dust jacket of *My Mother: Demonology* promoted it, "Yearning to discover who she is, to better understand herself, Laure embarks on a journey of self-discovery...." *Don Quixote* by Acker gets burnished as "an indomitable woman on a formidable quest." I journey then in a trip, from rhetorical figures as seen in her prose-narratives, skip off to an instance of explicating *poetry*. Acker applies the thought to words coming, to show how language itself can be on a reach, a rove for meaning, light up, in darkening in, seeking words arriving, in following on the heels as scripted, as it unfolds revelatory. In an illustration, this sheet of poem in her Papers:

This is a word
That will flower
Flower as
Sentences climb

And this thought
Won't stop thinking
As the air opens up
In time

And this hand will
Continue its breathing
As the worlds spin
And divide

And the picture that's drawn
In this silence
Will sing in
Silent lines.

55.

In one tribute after Acker's death, Diamanda Galás offers, "I once had a conversation with her late one night in Switzerland, and I was astonished to discover not only a provocateur but an extremely rigorous thinker with an encyclopedic knowledge of her craft." In another of my memories of the piece, or another set of remarks set down by Galás, she is wondering why she is only just now getting to know the woman. The account was displayed in one of the cases part of an exhibit of Acker manuscripts, drawings, and correspondences (curated by Brandon Stosuy, as "Discipline and Anarchy," November 7, 2002-February 1, 2003) for NYU's Tracey/Barry Gallery. Here I saw also first "Ten Out of Many Women Writers," a document I felt confirming in some of the connections I wanted to make with Acker. Sarah Schulman recalls how she and Acker went together to a Diamanda Galás concert. Though some might find German-Jewish-ness to be a particularly telling and emotionally productive route, and the patronymic she takes in distancing herself from one line does translate: field, I will not center my work upon it. Schulman, "To be born a German Jew is to feel entitled and endangered. She was born Kathy Alexander, the kind of German Jew that is known by real New Yorkers as 'Our Crowd'—her family, the Alexanders, along with the Lehmans, Loebs, Ochs, etc. were the best educated, wealthiest, and most sophisticated Jews in the world." Karen, not Kathy. In the last real book by my reckoning, *Pussy, King of the Pirates*, in "Alexandria" gets located a *most famous whorehouse*. There, inside: "The night is made out of yellow Jell-O. Diamanda Galás is performing this night. Oh, yes, I know her, I tell a few girls who're younger than me." A sentence that begins a part marked "Before the Days of Dreaming," opening the "O and Ange" section of the "In the Days of Dreaming" division of the book: "O, a woman and a Jew." "Alexandria," with the familial if slightly more mythic ring is found to operate as early as in *Blood and Guts in High School*, not only "that city of gold," a site with the stores of implicit pines that homeland riches might elicit (subconsciously or not) but also as a rife spot where Janey finds herself: *in gaol...for stealing two copies of Funeral Rites and hash from Genet.*

56.

How two or more entities link up creates a dynamic trailing across pages meant to be filling up like those of days for Janey do. She begins to play with language, to pass her days. Through the poems the character of Janey is writing, we see how she realizes she learns to construct her environment through not what is necessarily but only made through what focus isolates, how things connect only by not being other things (e.g. "(is not) (other) (a thing) (chair)" = "there is only a chair." There are not words for some things in some languages. "Janey hates prison," and depending on your standpoint, the textbook examples are not so innocuous. The verbs she is given to work with: to have, to buy, to want, to see, to come, to beat up, to eat, to rob, to kidnap, to kill, to know. Janey becomes the object of these verbs, subject to them (i.e. *to have Janey*, rather than have Janey have). She translates into her own English what aspects she chooses to emphasize, to intensify, prioritize, allow to gain in relevance. How will one represent notions of indefiniteness? The subtext blares seem apparent, once she tries to put herself back into a language of her own. In order to write "soul," to mark it out in the language picked up, there's a mark you must use, to precede the other marks, making the meaning of what all follows "immaterial." Also explored through "Janey," the written characters, is how one represents notions of indefiniteness.

57.

Acker herself was a student in language apprenticeships. There were parts of each she came across to home in on. She would work through the possibilities they offered or past the limits that their traditional instruction ingrained. Acker worked language in ways both philosophical and decorative. To learn another language outside of the mother tongue could supplement the environment one has been reared repressively in. Parents, in Acker, attempt to instill limits and take advantage of vanished horizons they impose. As *Blood and Guts in High School* puts it: *PARENTS STINK.* The movement into "The Persian Poems" section in this book begins with the lines: *WHEN SOMEONE'S IN PAIN, HE CRIES OUT,* emphasis conveyed throughout this book, like many of Acker's others, in all caps. "One day Janey finds a Persian grammar book. She begins to teach herself Persian." Captured by the "mysterious Mr. Linker" into his "white slavery business" (to mean sex slave), Janey, daughter, tries but ultimately will not be allowed to leave the preordained, societal rung, no matter how much she learns, turns and looks. Gender, as constructed through language, is shown to be a big part of this, as the farce of it both organizes and reinforces society. The learning of a new meaning-making system, as I read it, takes the time of many pages and exercises, but even in prison Janey reveals herself to be a bit of a self-starter. Agency would mean the body coming to terms for its own causes and effects and through them. "One day she found a pencil stub and scrap paper in a forgotten corner of the room. She began to write down her life...." Original ellipsis. Remember who holds her. Acker would short-circuit the loops of desire in her bids to dramatize what could be seen at the heart of the "functional" family. When your boyfriend is your father, there's no way he can be good. BLOOD AND GUTS: *I remember I wanted to be a good girl for my father.* She works inside the covers of this title with a literalism of Freud's family romance. Unless she's Hester Prynne, mommy is mostly a hindrance. Punctuated only by Janey's thoughts interacting with a new language she can use now to try to cry out in, the grasp is a solitary endeavor. We, reading along with Janey, encounter and learn about the *ezafe*, the Persian morpheme that *links two entities*, which displays some rhyme with the English *of*: "the night of Janey" would require it in Persian a book says. This linking unit is forgone with adjectives the language classifies as "deviant," places differently. Acker then extends the critique beyond America, New York City, New England, and English, as represented through Janey and her daddy as literature item. Janey goes to Tangier to find a coach there in another especial Acker favorite seeing the world through a sexual lens, Genet.

58.

What the novel might mean, that was something to begin translating, too. Acker did not just take it on board, and like it would in the midst of *Pussy, King of the Pirates*, the novel itself could conceivably become a map. Matias her executor would be somewhat right behind me, asking rhetorically, "What does her work *mean*? What is that which is now left in my care? A set of stories? No, more than this. A sensibility, a set of questions? Yes. A map, a documentation of treasure. Yes," in his "Cannibal Acker." Sometimes she can indeed be hard to follow. In *Pussy, King*, a section of the map also becomes a section of the book (inside a section of a narrative called "Playing House"). There we are for all intents and purposes reading over the narrator's shoulder or there behind those eyes, as we are told what we are looking at. I pause to reflect and am confounded by some, given a heading of "James Baldwin's Novel": a box of descriptive prose, carrying a sub-designation,

"Inside the book," is divided up into levels by separating dotted lines. This may be an attempt to track how one society is policed. *Ange lucidly believes in the progress of this country.* One of the notations graphs how in the top tier "no blacks" are seen. As the characters, the section's narrator and companion Ange, return, inside the book to the insides of the map on the next page, I will come back here. On the next page is another vantage, reading for this portion of the map another line of travel that moves both to the right and to left, *light at the end of the tunnel,* following the arrow signs, and another arrow points to a caption ("I'm simultaneously terrified/ and in wonder and I can/ never tell anyone this is/ happening") for the drawing, down from the BLOOD between HEART and PRISON. Between the two and also in the preceding scale of map is a kind of echogram, sketching out blood streams through the heart, words imaging, her words a legend: that which magnifies, *this is the presences of the heart.* And: *This is a prison because it's a room of the heart.* Does Acker happen to be reading Baldwin, as she is writing? She gains an intelligence being inside another author's book. But not just any. A read by the character Ange is a way of making out what we have just been catching glimpses of, to see, surmise, to summarize and simplify I am sure the experience: "This is what it's like to be a black man in our society."

59.

Is it satire, or true cluelessness? This comes out of nowhere, and a sense of meaning is lost or imposed. We cannot imagine what it is like, or if we believe we might, we do not then live the reality of it. How naïve is the Ange character, she of that foregoing conclusion? What does she really see when she looks at the map she has been reading, when she tells the narrator what she does? The narrator has hazarded if criminals are seen as not human, then this must be what a posthuman world would look like. Really, what does Acker mean when she asserts to Rickels "a woman of color like me"? Meaning for her, in the same breath: *Jews have only been passing as white for centuries.* How historically grounded does she believe this to be? Theoretically? And where between do the two begin to cleave. This may be disputed, but I would never want to tell her what she is or was. In the same source, Acker also elects this designation: "I'm so queer I'm not even gay." Her last novel, *Pussy, King of the Pirates*, would predate the rise in formalization of such understandings as the current fashion of intersectionality. Some occupations co-exist. In an early, uncollected review of Robert Louis Stevenson's work, and praising the older man's prose, young Baldwin shores the evaluation up by recourse to bemoaning the "nymphomaniac," among others ("the clotheshorse," "the fisherman"), who have now been "equipped with typewriters and entered the world of letters," before going on to further note the women who trouble—Baldwin's word is *darken*—the worlds of more successful Stevenson setups, as in *Treasure Island* and *Kidnapped*. Janey Smith, in another captivity narrative, picks up a pencil for stretches of *Blood and Guts*. In *I Dreamt I Was a Nymphomaniac*, there is one real Black Tarantula, an American Indian "sentenced to five years to life imprisonment for first degree burglary." Chris Kraus in her Acker book relates a moment where Kathy is in her journal writing of having gone to court after a bust around the sex show. She notes her minority status there. Of the disproportionately arraigned,

187

detained, the supposed "criminals": *may they live forever*. In the *Nymphomaniac* book, while "poisoners run loose," "every hippy and black person the cops could find on the scene of the crime are jailed." In the piece "Lust," a black man will take the rap for a murder the narrator has committed. That same narrator: "I didn't feel guilty because I had murdered a Jew." In *Empire of the Senseless*, it is a world where if you work for the government you supposedly are not then seen as *black*. In this same book, Harlem is narrated as the place where the black hates the Jew; the black is characterized as hating the Arab too, "cause Arabs started the black slave trade." Acker adds Arabs to the analysis of neighborhood relations flesh-and-blood Baldwin began in his essay in *Notes of a Native Son* (see "The Harlem Ghetto"). But where is *she* in all this, her *I*? (And pace Tom McCarthy in his "Infidel Heteroglossia" on Acker, how might that differ from a materialism of her body.) In *My Death My Life by Pier Paolo Pasolini*, a parenthetical, stage directions or an ironic, authorial or narrator aside goes: *All these distinctly different verbal elements go together because nothing makes sense anymore and this is an act of hatred*. Is this triggering a discussion or one upping, talk amongst "friends"? In her *Don Quixote*, Schön a glossing creator character tells us "is now rich, believes he owns the world," "surveying his room: the world," sees his situation of his traitor creation turning against him as analogous to "when England deigned, out of the goodness of his heart," to colonize and exploit for "decent social products" "then their human products turned on them devilishly and are still turning on them devilishly..." In *My Mother: Demonology*, President Bush the first says to wife, "I don't know why these people don't keep to their own race." Reagan either is just playing the part acting complicit in black death or really is—and I would add in AIDS—back in Acker's *Don Quixote*, while another speaker is stumping for Prince for free world leader, but it is the *My Death My Life* book which may be her most sustained attempt at deconstructing race relations, colonial and by extension American. There an Al'Amat ("I'm not black; I'm Irish," he tells Queen Gertrude) character appearing now in a dissection of Shakespeare's *Hamlet* self-identifies as Rebecca. James Baldwin, debating with William F. Buckley, Jr., Cambridge 1965, delves into subjugation and the destroyed sense of reality, seeing only *the white* as that which one is supposed to be, and a shock in the realization of a misrecognition of a scene. He says, "Gary Cooper killing off the Indians when you were rooting for Gary Cooper... [to discern then that] the Indians [all along had been] you" (See *I Am Not Your Negro*). To realize that the whole system of reality has not evolved any place for you. *A woman like me*, Acker says. The various levels of her *Pussy, King of the Pirates* map are a surface (outside), an inside (next level), and a third about a "heart" that is trapped inside. Acker's Shylock (*My Death My Life*) constructs the defense that because he loved a black man first above all others [like me] how could he be hostile? Nothing feels a perfect fit. He still sees a color. EMPIRE: *Though I'm not black, Harlem, I know your rancor, I know on what your hatred's fed.* This character's condition? Arab and female. In drawing distinctions, that state of being is something that language teaches.

60.

In a foreword to one of Samuel Delany's enterprises in the realm of sci-fi (*Trouble on Triton*), Acker constructs a dialogue with his work, to relate, that is not one of the white and black, but moves into questioning his feeling of what his chosen genre here can give above and beyond, in what it is pitted against. The fight becomes for her the opposition to that need to restrictively name: say *realism* of the *bourgeois*. Other classes are being held outside the control of meaning. Meaning webs. Acker steps so far in her appreciation for the Delany title, that carves for her a path in "literary geography," between novel-writing and poetry, as to pronounce every author Orpheus, every author searching for love, every poet a revolutionary. In his essay for *Dangerous Liaisons: Blacks, Gays, and the Struggle for Equality*, Delany searches amongst identities in other ways, how they become calcified, cemented, lead to reifications in violence, to formulate: *The difficulty of speaking about the relationship between the oppression of one sex by the other is the fear that the oscillating system of exploitation of women, white and black, by black men and by white, that alone is what allows race to be, will be revealed* ("Some Queer Notions About Race"). In Acker's *My Death My Life by Pier Paolo Pasolini*, her Shylock shares: *People have been dumping on me all my life and I never had a chance. I'll tell you what it's like to grow up in The South: If you talked to a black, you were scum you were black! If you liked a black, you were scum you were black! If you dared to read a book, you were scum you were black! If you wanted to go to a play, you were a fag!* And Antonio's response: *So you had no choice: you were black or a fag*. In the matter of the map that launched midstream in Acker's pirate book, though, there are other "colors like I've never seen" (PUSSY): *deepest, darkest reds*.

61.

Part of Acker's plan and one I hope to share some part in through writing on her work, textual contours, her wild calls to intellectual arms, is to somehow redress understandings of a life by troubling the more traditional coordinates of knowledge, to make these for us more permissive, less constrictive, to revalue that which has been stripped of all meaning but meaning made with one over another. When one term is set in opposition to another more readily, normally more privileged, in chains of signification that construct Western metaphysics, and Cixous traces it this way in "Sorties: Out and Out: Attacks / Ways Out / Forays," a process of undervaluation is stamped. If the male gets activity, sun, culture, day, if male is the head of the family, intelligible guard of the logos, if his work has form, is convex, steps forward, makes progress, seeds, you might take another route, she unabashedly then suggests. Let us have the options. Psychologically, socially, politically, in Acker, we will never be far from working and reworking definitions of who is normal, who has value, who is abominable and how and why, who is sick and who is sane, who should be confined, who is made to feel they warrant space, how, who belongs and who doesn't.

62.

If language and the limits of its rules are presented as fundamentally implicated in those characterizing perceptions Janey has at hand in *Blood and Guts in High School*, allusion creates for the récit a further dimension. This is especially true in a book like Acker's *My Mother: Demonology*. The concerns are pointed, as are her designs. Bataille, Georges, is ciphered in various ways throughout. One punning section gets headed "A

BAT AND I BECOME FRIENDS." He will underwrite Acker's narrative, just as he bolsters lover Laure's poetic legacy. The entirety of chapter seven is set under his imprint, in sharing the title of a work of his, "The Dead Man." The Tarot cards spread opening the chapter provide small consolation: *From these I learned that I'm a dead man, devoid of desire.* We see here the "Card That Names the Problem" (Ten of Swords, stabbed in the back), the "Cards That Tell What Will Happen If I Follow My Helpers" (in Acker, supporters of her work, as well as the authors who guide and whose books set precedents for her own, bed partners—often providing her with character, or scripts to follow like those in *Don Quixote*, which she then inflects—as well as those she turns to for the fodder for her own explorations and visions, those which she can *pulp*: the Victorian Dickens, or Cyberpunk of William Gibson—into whom she hacks in a setup (*Empire of the Senseless*). There are the "Cards That Name the Helpers," like Jean Genet, appearing in *Blood and Guts in High School*, to whom I like Acker will return. *My Death My Life by Pier Paolo Pasolini* not only begins with this author named for, but it is also dedicated to Pasolini in the book's end. Rimbaud and Faulkner trade off parts, *In Memoriam to Identity*. "Cards That Name the Present" and "Cards That Name the Immediate Present" are also given in the chapter opening of *My Mother*, as well as "Cards That Tell What Will Probably Happen."

63.

German had been my parents' language, we are told in the I GO BACK TO SCHOOL section of the third chapter, "Clit City," of *My Mother: Demonology*. When this element is introduced as part of the words then composing the book, it is with nothing like Janey's translations, helping us to read what might be strange to our eyes, no matter how liberal the equivalencies accompanying those Persian patches in *Blood and Guts*. No crib sheet anywhere within *My Mother*'s pages when it comes to German. (The Farsi here though is another story....) Five sections of German poetry interrupt the book's English. The copyright page provides the untranslated words are from Ingeborg Bachmann's "Lieder auf der Flucht" ("Songs"—of or in, it has been rendered elsewhere—"Flight"). The first German passage appears in the midst of the author's German tour. "According to the promoters, the tour's purpose was to present new American writing to Germans." After a discussion of loneliness, that comes in part from occupying a car with a playwright who speaks no English, and "being lost on roads I had never known and cannot name," the first bit we get is the second stanza of part VI of Bachmann's fifteen-part poem. While I oar through the translations I have procured, I also do not want to neglect how such stretches of silence, for, and of, Acker's English have a force that pools its own meaning between, among, lost equivalencies. As Bachmann tells us, "initiated into love," only here, or we are to know it first here. Lava bolts down, or spills over, Acker's character bottled up uncomfortably in the car, that voice absent for eleven Bachmann lines that pour in the pages. Lava, linked to entering love, is personified with "breath" by Bachmann translators agree; expulsion reaching, or hitting; such matter of degrees reminding me of Acker's method for her own translating—marked also by her at times as rewriting—as in a note to herself on a copy of a poem by César Vallejo, in her Papers, to *Make more FIERCE AND MAKE SEXUALITY*

STRONGER. ("Make more and more like a painting," a scene in *My Death My Life* is preceded by.) The Bachmann crater, spent now or exhausted, surrenders finally or reveals *the key—* to, for—"these locked bodies." Other undoubtedly attractive aspects of Bachmann's poem for Acker would be its pastoral scenes of an idealized childhood, held up in distinction to "walls," "gaol," and "lonely sailor hands." The mother, Acker writes in her essay "Seeing Gender": "as if she's a map, she's the key to my buried treasure." The bodies in Bachmann's poem are figured as rooms or chambers we enter and illuminate or light. The body, I would add, can be like a book obviously in this regard.

64.

"The Fire Sermon" section in *My Mother: Demonology*, of the seventh chapter, "The Dead Man," which contains within it seven sections and where all of the untranslated fragments of Bachmann's German appear, opens with an unsigned epigraph: "When lovely woman stoops to folly and / Paces about her room again, alone." Traced back on *My Mother*'s credits page to Eliot and *The Waste Land*: he uses his notes there to direct readers to another book, Eliot's lines in part from somewhere else, too. His lines' beginning are pulled from the song the character Olivia sings in Oliver Goldsmith's novel *The Vicar of Wakefield* (subtitle: *A Tale, Supposed to be written by Himself*). After a line, set off as a quote, but without any accompanying attribution—"No new world without a new language" (Bachmann, found on my own)—comes a second section in Acker's work from the Bachmann poem being sourced. Forgoing an arguably maternal image of breast and sea conjoined, Acker starts this time three lines into the second stanza of Bachmann's part VII, quoting the next five lines: your hips are landing pier or quay. My ships returning or coming home from a voyage too long or journeys too far. Happiness twines a rope or weaves a silver chain to which I moored or attached lie. Georg, as a love interest is named, has earlier tried to explain to the touring author why he can't sleep with her—before we get more German. MOTHER: *He pulled my head into his stomach and placed his arm around me.* Acker picks up the poem where she left it off before: the tongue only fledgling or also nascent. MOTHER: *words kept getting lost in all I was seeing.* A Bachmann line about the flesh, "dein Fleisch melonenlicht," she lets taper off before the suggested enters coloring her own words, and Acker sets down ones on tears and the supreme weight of the other.

65.

English interrupts the German, to tell how the playwright releases the touring author with instructions to call him first thing tomorrow morning, as soon as she wakes up. Some lines of Bachmann's original are dropped up to the next: I conjure or charm melodies or tunes that would even enrapture, or charm even, death. The last instance of Bachmann in this book floats below, follows on the heels of, a line: "I'm discussing the realm known as *the loss of language*." That is emphasized in the original. Acker does not provide simply flourishes. The metaphysical pining to be found in Bachmann's verse is both given and occluded on its grounds. Pointed to as well here is importantly in fact how in the place of uninterrupted words of Bachmann, what we get are descriptions of American authors holding forth in Germany. Though she takes part, the author is obviously skeptical and describes her predicament as "ridiculous." The Bachmann quoting concludes: *It is not I.* Or: "I am not the one." *I am,* or, "It is I."

66.

Where Robbins's yachts were tied right up alongside the perused streets, where tourists with pockets now empty strolled, girls left to wash up once no longer attractive commodities—the tint of romance in it then giving way to harder socio-economic facts, as Acker sees detritus, undesirables. PORTRAIT: *they were fourteen years old or older and too old for the streetwalker trade.* Robbins's street with its smell of "fried eggs and pommes frites" is pushed through Acker's imagination to the transposed New York that gets represented by a waft of "dried cunt juice and piss stains." She downshifts, lands his scene into one of underlying squalor, resources further tapped. Living in a building that has "a boutique on the ground floor" in Robbins's setting becomes her retreating to *the dirtiest apartment building* for sex. The "more modern lock" is necessitated presumably by the sketchiness of the surroundings. Relative prosperity becomes a New York locale of "no lights in the hall." *Jackie* must be shocked by the state of affairs in the apartment she enters. PORTRAIT: "There was no other furniture besides an armless metal chair. A bathtub covered by a wooden board served as a table. I didn't see a toilet, only a sink." Acker paints over Robbins's more excusable, European bedsit what becomes for some a New York City standard of living. *'It's not much,' he said, 'but it's home.'*

67.

The commissioned opera "Requiem" proves unsuccessful as a libretto. This verdict from Grethe Barrett Holby, instrumental in commissioning the piece, is reached after two early workshops of it. Holby writes of an attempt to develop the piece as a play with music. At one point, scenes in the play that are called autobiographical would be juxtaposed with "fictional transpositions" of these scenes from Acker's published novels, the hope to "do so without losing the core of the piece." Acker, in her own statement on the inception, classifies the work as "a retelling or appropriation" of O'Neil's *Mourning Becomes Electra* (a trilogy of plays in "Homecoming," "The Hunted," and "The Haunted"). She calls O'Neil's cycle a "reversion" of Aeschylus's trilogy, the Oresteia. States: "Both *Mourning Becomes Electra* and *Requiem* are personal stories and yet they are not." This information accessed on the once-maintained, CalArts-hosted site *welcome [back] to oblivion*, now vanished.

68.

The dance of the stripper, Acker's, compromised, I differentiate from the medium of porn that one might enter into in her word-rhythms. The latter space of sexuality and exposure is by and large of the literate variety, or middlebrow works brought down to levels of more repressive premises to be found in them—deconstructed back into dynamics they hide where porn does not so coy play. I deem instructive some scenes from Bette Gordon's 1983 film, *Variety*, with a script by Acker. Reviewing it in *The New York Times*, Janet Maslin calls the screenplay "painfully underwritten." When *In Memoriam to Identity* is covered in that same organ, Acker is indeed punk,

the reviewer—whose name it does not please me to write—
says: if by that one means not knowing how to play one's
instrument. Acker tunes differently. But play, she does, poses,
fed back. Some comforts depose others in repossessing, re-
appropriating, pointing to the codes of comfortable, at-home
"realism," as for one and for all. As she says in her speech for
the "Artist in Society" Conference, "A difficult read, or listen,
is not a proper commodity." Some writers screen other values.
(The critic giving Acker a hard time in review goes on in his
career to adapt for screen an Oprah pick, and that is done
"straightforwardly," "adroitly pared down," for a product
"glossy" compared to the "wilder, angrier downhill spiral" of
the source book, ethnicity "one of the rough edges that have
generally been smoothed here" in showing Middle America,
to extract from, circle back to, Maslin.) Some want to dream
the interrupted read of fiction. Some in a workshop, no matter
the level, return to that one, old reliable saw: telling, not
showing. That is not too far of a cry for me really ever from
the school of "just shut up" and, yes, man: strip like you are
supposed to, give me what I want how, allow it to be made
of you what will within those expected, perceptional frames
ordinarily, blindly, unwitting further conceptions. In the
interview in *The Argonaut*, her laugh is important enough to
set down. "Since I don't support the status quo I don't write
in that method (laughs)." Furthermore: "My writing forces
readers into a position of being unable to identify with certain
identic structures, which is very disconcerting." One "I" has a
possible solution in *The Childlike Life of the Black Tarantula*:
"I'm not happy but at ease open only when I'm in drag." Or,
more brassily in the words of "Politics": *I hate giving these
fuckers spreads opening myself....* In her translation notes for

The Thesmophoriazusae, she emphasizes as a philosophy and a way of life "high camp, not low camp, grand tragic speeches: all those disguises as Perseus and Andromeda, etc." The reference would be clothing, costumes. When we open her books, we will either be pleased or not so by these harder pleasures to be found and worked, moved through here or relaxed into—we might like the way the books confront, challenge, complicate, or even confirm our own priors.

69.

Acker slots over into third-wave or post-feminist camps, both of which her work helped usher in. Within the sex industry, a kind of Marxist firsthand still smarts, and defenses get qualified. Once having entered her body onto the stripping market, in telling her own tales of what was seen, heard, but also felt, while working such a scene, Acker attempts to re-script. A stance on the commercial and surrounding sides of such adult business develops. No discrediting the minds of the women put into positions necessitated by desperations of finance. No clear lines to the turn-ons at times. *Variety* starts with Gordon's story and then Acker takes it further in collaboration. While "Christine" is working, sounds spill over into the lobby from sex films she has gotten a job selling tickets to, "oh, oh yeah, God, uh-ooh." Christine, on her cigarette break inside, paces around, up and down the stairs between the levels of the porn theater, while men exiting begin to cruise her, over sounds from the screens. "You're a whore, aren't you?" "I am a whore." Christine sits down and smokes and thinks, before going up the stairs to the projection booth, to get her check. In another scene, Christine begins to tell a love interest about her new job: how guys are

there in the morning, waiting to get in, after it's been Lysol-
ed. Christine then goes into recitation, telling a story of what's
usually happening on the screen, what the women up there
say, how they will stare, undress, say *fuck me*—a bit flatly,
unimaginatively, bit doll-babyishly, emptied out to a function
clueless. The man Christine tells it all to says how he's got to
go, see her later.

70.

On the "Ten Out of Many Women Writers" list, Acker calls
Austen, Sand, and George Eliot: "The Older Ones." None of
them turn up explicitly in Acker's major works, though she
does with Sand play around in the manuscript not published
until after her death, "The Seattle Book," pulled from her
archive. Her more contemporary selections include Hannah
Arendt, for "the melding of precise feeling and reasoning."
Most cherished by Acker, *Men in Dark Times*, she quotes
from in her 1995 essay for the MMLA, "Writing, Identity, and
Copyright in the Net Age": "When Arendt talks about story,
about narration and narrative, she is not talking about a *master
narrative*. She is talking about language as it moves from one
point to another point." There is irony in the fact that Acker
is writing on copyright for MMLA. She was threatened earlier
with a lawsuit over work that might or might not appear there.
An academic threatens action, if Acker undertakes publishing
a piece generated through their interview. Acker is defended to
the board in an outline of how an original idea of an interview
with Acker moved towards an idea of conducting a conversation
among equals.... Grand-standing, attempt to overshadow or
not engage central issues of Acker's current writing practice;

she had been forced to enter another's space, terrain, etc., not vice versa.

71.

If capitalism is a daddy system, one that lubricates itself over the bodies that just as well might be dead of daughters to be wives kept in check and in house, or elsewhere thumbed, she proposed a change of form, a change of function. To McRobbie: "I'm always destroying—the hell with the word deconstruction—rigidities, habitual meaning, habitual contexts." Early on in her career, it was the "schizophrenic" she embraced as a mode. PORTRAIT: *I became two people. I now think the worst disease of our time is schizophrenia.* Deleuze defined schizophrenia, literarily, as that which occurs when the art-body is separated from the political-body. Acker plays the writing in many different registers, none of which she owns as her own, ultimately, though they always pass through her body, or a reflection of it, and are subsequently changed by her body—its past history and circumstances, current predicaments. A "fight against the fathers," as she calls it talking to Lotringer, will not lead to a finish of well-defined products which might be easily circulated within a current system of already existing markets.

72.

Alliances and self-designations are contingent upon those contexts within which they are formulated and always up for debate. My presentation of the discursive valences that may be found within Acker's voice of shifting authorities I would like to read is a readjustment, in contradistinction placed to any more totalizing account of them or her, where theory is applied to her work, fiction though it may be, a philosophy of the novel as possible poetry. (A video dated 1977, after reading from *Kathy Goes to Haiti*, in Canada, Western Front: "Now and then I write poems for my poet friends in New York." Before she begins "Raw Heat," she says she wrote it for a roommate, a present for this guy who puts music to her *songs*.) Criticism should not be allowed to top the performance in anyway. She taunts. I should note too just how invested in the dramatics of herself as "bottom"—or for those who may be less comfortable with such queerly theoretically defined positions and personalities, then in herself as *woman*—life and work proves to be. The older she and her work get, the more resistances coalesce in a formulation of the difference between "childhood" and *wonder* and the dead world of mastery of adult norms. No less important to her, thus to me, than how Acker comes to see in the world her work would be how she keeps coming-traveling, through and with it to try to see new selves, as old ones are lost in growing-evolving. I seek and point and pull out some of the base notes from which Acker and narrative proceed, though I want to be clear that I am aware my focus selects a frequency it preserves. You might try to open up and out—take a position of further lighting out—to feel continuity in and not confinement by that trace of Derrida, associating further Burroughs's exploding ticketed lines, letting the *little a*'s rock in waves, to dally with them all. None of them are taken completely on board, though relied on from time to time, strapped on, even. As in "Lust," where she writes: *Cut off a leg and another limb grows stronger.*

73.

Maya Deren, placed on the list ("the contemplative and the doer; join. She herself is a model for me") is in Acker's work, *My Mother: Demonology*. The reference is in passing, but she gives her her own, whole sentence: *At my brother's house I met artists. Romare Bearden. Maya Deren. This hint that it was possible to live in a community other than my parents', a community that wasn't hateful and boring, one of intellectuals, by opening up the world of possibilities, saved me from despair and nihilism.* If not Cixous, if not Kristeva, we will see Irigaray on the list: "theory leads to passion." She calls upon her in three of the essays collected in *Bodies of Work*— Acker's title entwined with one of Judith Butler, *Bodies That Matter*. Acker creates the twinship of sorts by citing from it plentifully in "Seeing Gender." Acker describes reading the Butler essay through its anthologizing in another volume of essays, *Engaging with Irigaray*. Acker employs Irigaray to read Sade and in her Colette essay, quoting there from Irigaray's *This Sex That Is Not One*, and potentially lending further psychoanalytical dimension to Acker's seeing herself reflected in Colette's work. "Female sexual awakening is a process of traveling rather than of arriving coming and stopping." I find the names to open my eyes, in a grant of new permissions. The "Ten Out of Many Women" list was one of the first things I looked for to see again in visiting Acker's archive at Duke University. The importance for me was a new way to approach Acker's work, as it seemed to me mostly confined, maligned even, dispensed with most readily by the almost solely dispatched Burroughs, a complicated relationship, to be sure. 11/18/1996: *main thing is/was the visit with William… the whole Kansas visit meant so much to me, Ira, my lineage.*

To her surprise, during this time, she finds Burroughs "open and openly kind (he's always been kind but scary to me on the surface)...he hugged me again and made an effort to speak to me despite my ridiculous shyness."

74.

Acker calls Arendt "the real tradition of humanism," and that comes up for Acker elsewhere. In writing on the prolific, academic and paraliterary Samuel Delany, she concludes: "By choosing the novel as an area for conversation, Delany is revealing himself as a great humanist." In her interview with Lotringer: "If you scratch hard, you find that I'm a humanist in some weird way. Well, humanist, you know what I mean." She trusts he does. "You had to start constructing," he answers, reading the move that Acker made in developing new strategies for narrative after her *Don Quixote*. She is leery of such summation. "Construction sounds very positive. People say, Oh, you're not so negative anymore. (Groans)." Other *contemporaries* on the list of "Ten Out of Many Women": de Beauvoir, Christa Wolf glossed, "Her praxis is that of the Ismael of Moby Dick." With an extra "o," Christa *Woolf* makes an appearance in Kraus, in a section of *I Love Dick* beginning, "Here are some notes I made about schizophrenia." "In Felix's book *Chaosophy* there's a great discussion on schizophrenia between him, Deleuze, and eight of France's leading intellectuals. All of them are men." "I was at a dinner at Felix's loft with my husband, Sylvere Lotringer." "Sylvere would moderate a live discussion between Felix and Tony and the German playwright Heiner Muller. They needed one more speaker." "'What about Christa Woolf?' I asked." "Finally the communist philosopher Negri graciously replied, 'Christa Woolf is not an intellectual.'"

75.

Duras, also from the list, is arguably the model for "MD," one of the *girlfriends* in Acker's *Pussy, King of the Pirates*. A couple of allusive, or buried if you like, jokes directed around this character include a reference to being *dry* ("never touched a drop of the stuff") and a *gift* for violent eruptions (she "kicked a fish"). I go to Duras's scandalous story "Albert of the Capitals," where the author notes in preface of the fictional setup, "Thérèse is me. The person who tortures the informer is me." The author's queer companion in her last years, Yann Andréa, might lend to Acker the character, too. *M.D.* is his account of one of Duras's hospital stays, after she has nearly drunk herself to death. Andréa rhymes himself in ways in the text of Acker's life: Matias Viegener, MV. After stating how a sense of solidarity between herself and Viegener has been established through disliking the same people, in her "Kathy's Stuff" essay Bellamy confides to him (and the listener, reader) the contents of an email she received shortly after the 2002 conference at NYU. "*Matias was very odd. He seemed to have no self. He was like the fag valet of the great diva who only lives for her.*" Viegner smartly answers her back: "There were so many EGOS walking around that weekend, they didn't need mine added to the mix." I quote from a manuscript in my possession. With Duras and Acker though, the influence of the former on the latter's enunciating, compare "*crucified from within to all that's intolerable in the world and proud of it*—that's my kind of writing" as in *Pussy* to the mother's philosophy in Duras, as stated in her text (a story turned into both a play and later a film), in "Whole Days in the Trees": *I can understand everything that hunger and poverty make you do—that's my brand of intelligence.* It comes in a moment of bonding after the mother's son's current girlfriend has hinted she's been forced to resort to prostitution in the past to survive. *The Burning Bombing of America*: "I go to Grand Street to give B. a book [ ] *Destroy She Said*" (Duras). Acker sums up this love and affinity on her list with: "We whose psychologies are made by outer circumstances or politics, who are distorted in and by a society whose nature is such that we are from our births apart, we are forced to consider our obsessions."

76.

I visited "Kathy Forest" at New York's White Columns gallery, January 10, 2007, Bellamy's exhibition of parts of Acker's wardrobe loaned by Matias. With the piece generated around the installation, "Digging Through Kathy Acker's Stuff," *stuff* does at least double duty. QUOTE: *As everybody else is scooping, Matias and Connie Samaras, who were with Kathy when she died, tell how they removed Kathy's piercings before she was sent to the crematorium. 'The one in her labia was Kathy's favorite piercing.' These intimacies are revealed with a tone of reverence and a disarming matter-of-factness. Matias and Connie poking around in a dead woman's genitals with no acknowledgment of the strangeness of the image—that is so Kathy.* Emphasis on the *so*, Bellamy. As another segment of the circuit, Samaras has produced a piece, part of a larger project, in which the end of the living, breathing performance come to be known as Acker is structured I see pretty much as apotheosis. A facet I underline from Samaras is the observation: *Tenderly your hand rests on your current favorite stuffed animal, a ferret.* The piece is made possible in part with a series of selections from Acker's last notebooks, given a title, "The Birth of the Wild Heart." MV shares. Quotes in pieces from Acker primary sources indicate a notebook in common, at least one, which both Samaras and Kraus write of and use, both writing too of how it came to be in their possession. Matias writes to me: "I've known for a while that you were working on KA & it makes me happy."

77.

The bed, or the cradle, the lesson, or the lens is in the book. It is where Acker will live now. In another title where the plan was to be an Orpheus to her own "I," done it before, looking back is partly what the narrative concerns itself with, *My Mother: Demonology*, the second part, "Out (In the Form of Healing)": Acker has a chapter entitled, "Redoing Childhood." Chapter seven has a section that introduces an idea of *redreaming*. It is true we must see here in part "red," and then the rest of the word. The "Clit City" chapter of this book, inside of which *lit*erature is in some ways always, includes a section "Preparation For The Unmentionable Based On A Pun." Puns in Acker are in dimensions both of the aural and visual, suggestive, echoing. Acker writes in *My Mother*: "In the first class I took, a class about theory, the teacher told us about the works of the novelist Juan Goytisolo. Goytisolo uses plagiarisms (other texts) in several ways: sometimes his characters read, discuss, or see other texts. Sometimes two simultaneous texts compose the narrative. Sometimes Goytisolo changes someone else's text in an attempt to contaminate and subvert something or other. Count Julian," Acker begins, then continues, the subverting and contaminating herself: "I mean Goytisolo." She is to underscore through her play at "slippage" the sense of her own irony. Acker was well aware just how often the singer would be confused with the song, is invited to be. She knows she herself can be and might be read as, for just one number, *Janey*. Or she is more like Laure now.

Acker goes on in the panegyric to Goytisolo's prior example with a relation of how he "subverts, invades, seduces, and infects all that's abhorrent to him by transforming the subject into an empirical self, a text among texts, a self that becomes a sign in its attempt at finding meaning and value." Now I blatantly point out how Acker has just done it, this very deed, increasing the complication of Goytisolo's text by making it just another text among her many. Acker, if one has been paying attention, she seemed to want to scream, appropriates all of his techniques, and how, as she further takes Goytisolo for herself, in the cited lecture. She concludes the quote from this theoretical teacher: *All that is left is sex alone and its naked violence.*

78.

Her books get stuffed, too, like her animals in many senses: with poems, diary accounts, passionate interests. Books enter each other in Acker's books, through Acker's hands. Inner workings of narratives change dimensions. To get through the next door, she would do what she must do. Like Carroll's Alice does, she sees what happens when following directions. Acker sets down another bottled name, or idea, offering, to size, book, poem, song. At the end of *Blood and Guts in High School*, in "The World" section, after Janey our protagonist dies Catullus is invoked. "A second of time," a bold typeface, subscript to the announcing of her passing in the passages above, underscores. This unit of meaning suspends there on the page, all the reader is left with, before "The World" division opens, on the next, facing page. "The World" movement is an inset section detailing the creation of and expiring of consciousness. It is not listed on the book's table of contents page. Pictures are drawn and labeled by accompanying sentences that more pictures interrupt in "The World." *The most important book on human transformation is hidden with the corpse Catullus in the Saba Pacha Cemetery in Alexandria*, followed next in the sentence by a pictogram, a black box, a book, followed by concluding, *because all books were written by dead people*. A square mark of an arched façade is identified in "The Journey" subsection as "Catullus' Tomb," pointed out from a surrounding maze. "Dead Catullus" wakes and tells a story of boxes within boxes within boxes, of setting out for the East River. There are no page numbers on these pages. Numbers resume with the last page of the book in our hands, following a panel illustration keyed, "So we create this world in our own image," and a section "So the doves…"

79.

The archive of her papers at Duke University contains a practically inaudible cassette tape of Acker and a British astrologer discussing her chart. Her actual faith in the elucidating powers of such a system is further substantiated by another document related to her life, this one in the Serpent's

Tail/High Risk Archive. Here Acker notes the zodiacal implications for the twelve writing students she has before her at one time. Some of my particular favorites: "lion aristocrat" and "weird sex." In terms of Acker's own personality morphs in her earliest works interesting is "hidden criminal depths" for another. A student has a set of thinking powers as well as a need for guidance. Another student is *perfect. analytic, precise.* Another is "cute." As well as rewarding navigating a classroom is a potentially fraught experience: "BEWARE (Scorpio 3X-Cancer rising)," "abstract-intellectual, lost. underneath, hidden stubbornness." Acker goes into what she calls in correspondence "zuzuland" when she teaches. Looking forward to meeting up with one of her publishers and friends in Kansas, she suggests, "We can go searching for delinquent students again." Rimbaud is made one by virtue of *In Memoriam to Identity,* as is Acker's "Laure" character in *My Mother: Demonology,* Janey in *Blood and Guts in High School.* A book report on *The Scarlet Letter* by Janey begins: *We all live in prison. Most of us don't know we live in prison.* Hester, with whom the author relates "wouldn't be quiet and hide her freakiness like a bloody Kotex" and "was as wild and insane as they come." It is perhaps Pearl the child though that Acker identifies even more with, *also* characterized, "as wild as they come," "makes no distinction between what's outside her and her dreams," and one who will: *open herself up she is soft and totally hurtable that's what being wild is.* Acker goes on, "Hester's husband's a top scholar. A scholar is a top cop 'cause he defines the roads by which people live so they won't get in trouble and so society will survive."

80.

The partners in crime the two young lovers become live in the house of the Alexanders, bearing that name of Acker's own troubled birthright, they of the surname she carried once before first marriage to some told wrong stock. It is the acquired name she keeps and under it that her publications begin to move, push forward the vision of characters of women and girls always also taking up with the wrong types. This is especially so once the gender of her narrators, in the wake of the Tarantulas predating more involved structural games and plots, get ironed out. Such play does not really come back full-swing until *Pussy, King of the Pirates*. Webs get swept more up into novelistic floor plans, walls that were there now nested within. PORTRAIT: *the walls of my fantasies.* In the inbred interiors, there are windows onto and into individual consciousness and the others that they come to hold: those of characters, the cultures outside them, a reader called to synthesize them all together or not, as viewer or receiver only, insider or outside of how one's self continues. Citations and interactions multiply over and through the writing. Character in Acker's books is often constituted in part from characters from other books that bring with them some of the characteristics they hold outside of a present bind. The characteristics can be complicated then, as they are slyly, or not so, dealt with by the character of the book into which she has inserted the outside influence. What I mean to say is how Acker is fucking around with what is being used this time to compose writing—why and how included characters are being grafted in? Underhanded, or overt, depending on the moment in time, depending on the book, depending on mood, rhetorical developments furthermore get complicated by the fact that characters of a supposedly "flesh and blood" variety are not the only place where Acker trains re-limning focuses. Symbols, settings, words themselves gain a kind of *character* in Acker. She works selected ones up into the privacy of codes. A movement of language is addressed, dressed and undressed, as she camouflaged and spotted story in new coats. A supplementary, side drama in any of her books, just as much as any sex, just as much as the life being narrated, exposed, is the poetics that Acker would make of her own knowing repetition compulsions.

81.

In *The Burning Bombing of America*, she makes a two-legged signifying chain in a conjoining of EXPERIMENTS-JOURNEYS. To McRobbie: "Decentralization is absolutely major to me," Acker says of her pursuit of the non-hierarchical, a political disruption which she sees as not taken generally to be a focus of post-modernism in Anglo-Saxon culture, an oversight she says not surprising. Pinpointing our stable grounds of knowing she would have shift in the nexuses she won't separate—like *HEART-SUN,* and *earth-sky,* both also of *The Burning Bombing.* Not quite equating, no, but making a new forming through: "thing-being," "Women-Men," "cat-children," "desire-fur." Here too women turn into cats, cats "mother": *I serve a Cat [ ] I lick Her nipples continuously.* AMERICA: *there are no families [ ] but centers [ ] warm breast.* I think of her pet name. As prominent as humans here are numerous other options with which to identify: lions, elephants, deer, monkeys, dogs, goats, squirrels, birds of all sorts, and giraffes, the last a main character of desiring in another early, unpublished work signed by The Black Tarantula. That piece,

"Voodoo," opens: *In Haiti, there are many animals.* "Giraffe doesn't need to boss around other giraffes and get bossed around by other giraffes." "Giraffes fuck incredibly.... Horny all over." Animals exist in a more plentiful and generating realm: "I'm going to travel and travel and see everything. I'm going to run with the animals with the wild biting horses and antelopes who run so fast they seem to fly their hoofs don't touch the grass especially the thin gazelles cats and lions and tigers who let me pet them as we run, huge black wolves"—no lone, big, bad one is standing out here all alone—"nothing hurts me; at first I can't move very fast but very soon I learn to keep up with the wild animals, running effortlessly over smooth slowly rising and falling plains covered by grass, running and running and running." She writes this, words this, after a dying father is left in a hospital by her character in the first, unpublished, "Blood and Guts in High School."

82.

It is not unforeseeable that the three acts of "Requiem" and the dreams and hospital drama of "Eurydice in the Underworld" would have met up between covers of a venture to expand to include as well other characters, further myths, happenings in Acker's life. Highly likely, if not for the end. Copious notebooks attest to the speculation. What we have here may be only a dim shadow of another not yet met evolving vision to enlarge, lodge, expound. As it is, "Eurydice in the Underworld" is an unclassifiable work if ever there was one for Acker. "The Overworld" section begins, after an opening epigraph from Algerian feminist novelist, scholar, translator, and filmmaker Assia Djebar (1936-2015) from a novel which Djebar subtitled a "cavalcade," with a first line situating us: *Fifteen years later*. The opening section is composed of nine parts that take divergent dramatic forms. Our sense of this setting of reality is mediated by stage directions, parts for characters, and lyrics to be sung. A good portion of the piece is seen to arguably exist in a second-person voice, as a story being told to in and narrated on the self, when Acker renders shorthand Eurydice's name and role at times with *YOU*. Penultimate parts six, seven, and eight are subdesignated "stations," with that final one further classified parenthetically: "death." Then Orpheus is wandering around outside the hospital asking, "Oh, where is Eurydice?" Signing how he's not quite all there in front of her anymore, or undecided, the point her *I* might drift to, if not *YOU*, Acker abbreviates also this other main character, OR. A work of concision in its Arcadia Books publication, page 14 is already part nine. Orpheus is answered by the piece stepping off its former stage, and followed by a *Diary written by Eurydice when she's dead*. I recall to you Acker's fear of being trapped in one. It starts, "I'm in the middle of dirt." *U-turn* is how Orpheus begins to refer to his partner once he's "returned to the realm of the living." Acker changes his orientation as he gets to walk away, from death, symbolically, lyrically again to her. By the end, she changes his life no longer being written as a play. He's taken out of the realm of real-time, further possible engagement with her. Her name, her fate, has been reversed, or sealed: supplemented by his decision. All of these with Acker. In another, earlier section, "Orpheus," comes the learning: "Maurice Blanchot says that Eurydice is the extreme to which art, Orpheus's art, can attain." Acker will try to go on in *letter found from Orpheus after his death*. "E" replies in a following section. Then a parenthetical reclassifies her response as a *poem*. More than that: "just one of the poems that dead girls can write to each other in memory of the life above."

83.

Acker's dream of hell here is filled with women bankers. Our "I" wants to take out a loan, but she realizes she will soon be tried. By becoming insane, the narrator believes she might escape being judged. In the "in the courtroom of the dead" section of *Eurydice*, we are given a map of a walk down a street that includes a *hole in reality*. In the "in the school of the dead" (see Cixous) section, there is another map, but "A picture of the Underworld," as it is labeled, is not much (escapist) consolation: courtroom, bank, two moats around houses that girls have been murdered in, desolation pictorially rendered in *the lonely complex of buildings, the judging table, the fires of hell.*

84.

All-caps emphasis in a manuscript in the Serpent's Tail/ High Risk Archive: THE ONLY GOOD THING ABOUT WRITING IS IT'S THE ONLY PLACE, OR TIME, YOU CAN TELL THE TRUTH. AND THEN YOU CAN TELL THE PERSON OR PEOPLE YOU'RE TALKING TO IT'S NOT THE TRUTH, I MEAN YOU DON'T WANT TO DUMP ANYTHING ON ANYONE, THIS IS ALL FICTION. A section of *My Mother: Demonology* identifies itself as "Bits From the Diary I Wrote in Germany—I Was Just Copying Porn

Novels." Life gets refracted through another word forum. A section of *Pussy, King of the Pirates*, "I Meet Myself," is given sub-designation "Pages turn out of my first school diary." After a parenthetical that claims *no date*, we go on to read: *school is a dairy / because all headmistresses are cows*. We are also to read as a section in this book, "From Antigone's Personal Diary": *so I just got out I upped and left put it however you want*—out from the life she was living, "schools" of thought she was running among. "Eurydice in the Underworld" contains a section entitled, "Diary written by Eurydice when she's dead." The logic here is at times dreamlike (for example, "Inside, two girls have just been murdered. I know this is true because when I look at them, they look like store-window dummies. Therefore, the same could happen to me or to any of the girls who are with me," and, emphasis in the original, "I *intuit*, that is I know, that the murderer's here.") Clues arise from or can go into the body itself, a diary of knowledge of words.

85.

Often the *porn* Acker uses is "erotica," perhaps a fine distinction, another rev, as when she cites Violette Leduc's book, the one that consists of scenes initially deemed too explicit in their depictions of lesbian sex and so subsequently removed and published alone, taken from part one—*La Bâtarde (The Bastard)*—of a projected but never completed four-part autobiography. *Mad in Pursuit* would be the second, less successful volume, one detailing Leduc's discovery by and fixation upon Simone de Beauvoir. Juan Goytisolo would give the heroine Leduc a rather scintillating documenting in the second volume of his own autobiography, *Realms of Strife*.

He refers to her "half-real, half-imagined attacks of madness and depression," her "terrible physical appearance" which has been documented, "her loneliness and isolation: she suffered or pretended to suffer from a persecution complex, but at times she would calm down and her vulgar face broadened into a cunning grin. She was a 'play-actress and martyr,' according to the expression coined by Sartre, and waxed ecstatic at the 'happy couple' of Monique and myself." Monique is Goytisolo's wife at the time. "She wanted me to pass on to her an old pair of trousers, 'with a drop of semen on the fly,' she said plaintively, since she lived alone, without a man, and that souvenir of me would warm her up a bit." Goytisolo further dishes Genet: in one dramatic remonstrance, knocked over the woman's supper table because he did not want to eat when she insisted he must what she had prepared. Goytisolo then says that Genet, whose destiny Goytisolo admits himself *obsessed* with and in the same letter where he reveals himself to his wife as homosexual, that letter also included in the autobiography, was one of the two passions in Leduc's life (the other another gay). The three authors strike various chords in her, as they provide precedent and example in aestheticized registers for Acker's own disclosures.

86.

In *Politics*, as the narrator speaks of her time in the scene of the strip-sex-show, far from being viewed as some positive, fulfilling experience, Acker writes: *they don't want to see anything but dead cunt.* The promise of sexual liberation isn't found working in such a place like that, but rather, as time goes on, in a promise—"self-sufficiency," or call it mockery, bands of punk women strapping-on, packing, as she discusses in an interview with R. U. Sirius after *My Mother: Demonology* and on the path to *Pussy, King of the Pirates*. Those mock-ups sported in public will be just as effective. *And the only thing guys have to learn is that there's nothing wrong with dicks and cocks, but don't think you've got the only cocks in the world.* Just as effective another point for entry, gladly made travesty of that which had been lorded over one in the past (not taking it off, but putting it on, a flip to Burroughs's penetrable species of boys from other planets), turning their own on. A repressed that will not stay that way, what Acker makes of the public strip often returns within the context of her fiction, but she would not only assert and use it there. In some interviews it would also be called upon, alluded to in some book reviews, conceded to as a knowledge of the world that Acker speaks. As a mode of knowing, it would rear as well its head in her essays. It comes as part of the mating dance in *I Dreamt I Was a Nymphomaniac* with her Peter character, "capable of deceiving both sexes," who in his "long white silk skirts with thin nets of white and snow shaws" "looks both like a female faun and like a young boy who adores to tease" (in *The Adult Life of Toulouse Lautrec*, "Peter's a lamb"). *I once worked in a sex show*, the narrator whispers. Some times, an early divide perceived between this employment and artistic ambitions Acker claims to pinpoint as the root of the very *schizophrenia* she then explored along formal lines in "Politics" and work before the making of her *Great Expectations* novel. She writes in *I Dreamt I Was a Nymphomaniac*, "No one but I knew of these two identities." The money needed to support a career is not yet come into in other ways.

87.

Becoming a silent complement, defaulting unwittingly to man's most gainful employment is part and parcel of the "lobotomy," which recurs regularly in Acker as shorthand for accepting the state of just the way things are. *In Memoriam to Identity*, Harry says, "She couldn't work as a stripper anymore because it was making her sick." In the same book: *Question: Why do girls become whores?* And, *Answer: A lot of girls do for a while. The ones who don't just for a while, die.* EXPECTATIONS: "Before she worked the sex show she had earned all the money she needed especially the money for all the medicines by starring, she was either the only one or one of two, in sex films. She had thought of earning her money this way because when she had gone to a top Eastern University a doctor friend had told her her face was ravishingly beautiful. She had gotten these beginning model jobs by looking in the back pages of the *Village Voice*." So Acker's work begins. You might note the movement of the signifier, as it loses its grounding in acceptable, social reality, a necessary journey? No way to stop sliding down a chain, from one school of thought on to the next, in being instructed on her beauty by a doctor (Ph.D.?), lead to modeling, i.e. "star" in sex films, a gateway to the live show, to an actual flesh model.

88.

The stripper's dance is a staging done to control a lingering childhood anxiety about stumbling upon what you don't understand. Now in one mother of a position, the open all night, there all night—will be one mother like no other. When Acker is stripping, she is stripping for men, fairly, in all honesty, I note, while proceeding to examine the relative positions of her set-up. Here the man-boy-child catered to in comfortable seat, believing he is controlling, he should be, all strings connected to bills as long as he has them to spend. He can see how she doesn't have what he possesses. This strip-show, sex show can be seen to function as the zero degree of sexual politics for much of Acker's writing, and it is from this position that Acker's sexualized aesthetic theories may be said to found the primary, anti-capitalist roots. Here is how the personal becomes her worldview, though through this perspective she by no means seeks to negate or censor the body. Rather, desire is to reclaim through the body an unchained self-definition not beholden to configurations of woman as purely familial or complementary to more publicly exonerated male positions. Janey only becomes "beautiful" in *Blood and Guts in High School* once she has demonstrated that she can: *make a man feel secure, desirable, and wild.*

89.

I can't honestly tell you how many times the word "cunt" occurs in the work. In the pieces making up the trilogy: at least 46 times. It is more like 54 times for the volume *Literal Madness*, probably over 26 times in *Blood and Guts in High School*, at least 15 times in *Great Expectations*, at least 22 occurrences in *Don Quixote* of the word, 44 times in *Empire of the Senseless*, 36 for *In Memoriam to Identity* I count, at least 32 in *My Mother: Demonology*, in the province of *Pussy, King of the Pirates* I easily see 25. It is a word that appears to name genitals (PORTRAIT: "skin separates from skin in my cunt," and "I touch my cunt with my hand"). It appears as identity, grounding, arguably (PORTRAIT: "my cunt is my center my cunt is my center my cunt is my center"), a place of vulnerability (PORTRAIT: "Kick me again in the cunt, please"), is elevated too, connotes prize, reward (PORTRAIT: "I don't want to become a secretary because I don't want to eat shit I want to eat cunt"), is derogatory (PORTRAIT: "You didn't bring me enough money today you fart-faced cunt"). Ophelia in *My Death My Life by Pier Paolo Pasolini* speaks it out: "Cunt. Tramp. Floozy. Flounder. Dead fish." It is a metaphor (PORTRAIT: "Park foliage squeeze open close like a voluptuous cunt." In her *Don Quixote* it is one too, "like the bliss of a throbbing red cunt dawn." *My Mother: Demonology*, "In the swampy regions of the cunt, Charon rowed and plied his boat as if the skiff was a finger." Or synecdoche (PORTRAIT: "Now that cunt's gone," and also in *Kathy Goes to Haiti*, "I know he doesn't care about me I'm a cunt he hates me." MOTHER: *So as soon as Dad woke up to a cunt, he kicked her out of his house*). Metonym, PORTRAIT: "Cunt special," or in *Blood and Guts in High School*, "My cunt used to be a men's toilet." It is societal oppression, in *High School*, where, "*Being in prison is being in a cunt*," or an exclamation of desire in the same location, "cuntcuntcunt." It is conceit, flourish (EXPECTATIONS: "you can't eat cunt, writing isn't a viable phenomenon anymore," and IDENTITY: "Perhaps outside where the swans are sitting are the cunts of the night"), construct of *Empire of the Senseless* ("On the other hand my construct (a cunt) and I had to find the code"), abjection in that same book, "Climatically Algeria is a sluggish country and cunt." *My Mother*, emphasis in the original, abjection there too where "she'll be unburiable—no dogs will stick their noses into this cunt—because the stink of rebellion that is named *menstrual blood*"). In *Empire of the Senseless*, the *objet petit a*: "In my heart of hearts or cunt I've always known what men want from me." This substitution of signification as well is performed in *Don Quixote*: "in her heart of hearts, or cunt." It's a subliminal state (*Empire of the Senseless*: "In a river. In my cunt"), stigmata (ibid: "Her red cunt was the center of the cross"), desiring machine (ibid: "For the cunt opens and closes, a perpetual motion machine, a scientific wonder, perpetually coming, opening and closing on itself into ecstasy or to nausea—does it, you, ever tire?"), plane of immanence, also EMPIRE: *Cunts open and close whether or not they're opening and closing on anything.* Mother Nature, creation (EMPIRE: "My cunt is a tree. Every leaf, every blossom, every fruit comes from my cunt..." original ellipsis), subject (ibid: "my cunt is also me"), conduit, element, knowledge (*the queen, the witch, who lights up her cunt in the pot of the earth, will never tell us what she knows*, when she is quoting-translating Rimbaud, and also in IDENTITY: "without memory, the meat, my cunt, rots"). In *My Mother*, "Father decided to make me the center of his portrait of New York. A crowd of males, including him, would stand around me. They'd set my cunt on fire." It is a confirmation—Stein's: "I am me because my little dog knows me"— (IDENTITY: *I'm not dead: I've got my cunt. I've got my cunt; it's not a hole; it's an animal and I love the animal*), or *méconnaissance* (IDENTITY: *Mother didn't put her cunt around loneliness and she suicided*). Or it transports (IDENTITY: "Cunt is perfume waft of freedom"), MOTHER personification ("Part of the cunt's mind thought, I want to get out of here"), organism ("Let your cunt come outside your body and crawl, like a snail, along the flesh"), in PASOLINI: "there's something provisional, fragile, something tenuous a seashell enclosing a skinless creature. A cunt"), an animating spirit (*My Mother: Demonology*, "The only way to raise the person from death is via the cunt"). MOTHER: "The cunt is always speaking," ideal-implication ("If Cathy was pure of cunt," ibid), color ("cunt-pink," ibid). A source in PUSSY, KING: "my cunt, the well where all is bottomless," or "Pandora's cunt," and also a dream symbol: "When her mother had died, a jewel case had been opened. The case, consisting of one tray, had insides of red velvet. O knew this was also her mother's cunt."

90.

In one of the classes I had with Eve Sedgwick, around "Non-Oedipal Psychologies," she gave us all a stapled gathering of photocopied pages, highlights selected by her from *A Dictionary of Kleinian Thought*, edited by R.D. Hinshelwood, including an entry on the history of the theoretical and the clinical use of the word "part objects." Though Melanie Klein would seem to be somewhat off Acker's radar—or it is telling that Klein's name is not mentioned or attacked in work in the manner Acker reserves for (the name of) father Freud—I believe she would have recognized her in due time, if not already, through Kristeva—set about perhaps disrupting or adding her own side of biographical knowledge as an in to Klein's formulations or Kristeva's interpretations. She may already be ahead of me. She works undoubtedly already *unconsciously* in Acker. Klein is cited in note number 16 for chapter four of Kristeva's *Powers of Horror*, where in this "essay on abjection" Kristeva is laying out conditions of the divisions in society underpinning symbolicity. Interestingly, surprisingly much is decidedly predicated on that one separation, high-low.

91.

In the later books, where Acker works primarily from her interest in "myth," she will have the character speaker role sign expand to more full-blown, all-encompassing storyteller function. Any pretense to authorial objectivity in the novel realm now being entered into is complicated by a formality of dramatics of marking. This character we are handed off to controls the character of the forming words, as clearly Acker pulls her strings through them. In *My Mother: Demonology*, there is very little to the book that must not be attributed to the mother in some way, with almost the entire bulk of its makeup "said" to issue from the mouth of the title character or conception. One single, short paragraph precedes a line ending—*My mother spoke*—in a colon, which will open us out onto the rest of the text of the book, taking us "Into That Belly of Hell Whose Name Is the United States," as part one is called. (Cf. *In Memoriam to Identity*, where, *I am my mother*, Capitol gives us in addressing 'round Rimbaud.) The first part of *Pussy, King of the Pirates* is labeled a preface and calls upon the characters of Artaud and O to speak it. As their existences are both invoked and evoked by Acker, these two voices for narration, with their "mythic" status, for Acker at least, trade off between themselves, orienting the reader, composing the book text, that design then giving way to Acker's orchestration of a story of her girl piracy. She ditches any pretense of a neutral narration, as in *My Mother: Demonology* and to a lesser degree in monologue of an historical character like Sadat in *Great Expectations*. She dispenses with objectivity, to overtly make character objects that do her narrative biding. These part-characters, the connotations they bring with them, announce and trouble "detachment." Characters like "O" and "Artaud" and "Anwar Sadat" exist in a shadowy limbo, by a number of shades, depending on what the reader knows before or only through the book. They present as much as they themselves are present being.

92.

In Acker's interactions with others outside of her books, she mentions some of the names now you might come to expect. In an interview in the magazine *Red Bass* (Ron Kolm Papers, Fales) there is Deleuze. "Kristeva's work is real important, Irigaray's in some weird way." Given Luce Irigaray's elemental rewritings of philosophy, as in *Marine Lover of Friedrich Nietzsche* and *The Forgetting of Air in Martin Heidegger*, it is a link that seems to me more than apropos. In the interview with McRobbie, Acker names Kristeva's *Powers of Horror* as a major work, and again mentions Irigaray. She acknowledges here a stylistic influence, primarily, though she concedes she also shares Irigaray's interest and investment in the body. A section of *My Mother* is entitled I hazard after Kristeva, "About Chinese Women." Allusions appear to Cixous's work, too. The section of "Eurydice in the Underworld," entitled "in the school of the dead," has its very likely originating source, both complement and complication in mirroring, in Cixous's *Three Steps on the Ladder of Writing*. Cixous postulates here that something or someone must die figuratively in order for good writing to be born. Who else but Cixous sparks the ire in *Don Quixote* when "Medusa" appears, "What the Hell do you know!" *screaming: Her snakes writhe around nails varnished by the Blood of Jesus Christ. 'I'm your desire's object, dog, because I can't be the subject. Because I can't be a subject: What you name 'love', I name 'nothingness.' I won't not be: I'll perceive and I'll speak.'"* Cixous's "Laugh of the Medusa" dates about a decade before Acker's taking the piss here. When Acker addresses the work of Richard Prince, she quotes from Cixous's collaboration with Clément. Cixous is specifically cited after Acker writes, "The fight against the patriarchal sexist society is the fight against the refusal to allow contradiction, difference, and otherness." You could take a bite from Cixous, some form from Kristeva, a swell too from Irigaray, as how Acker approaches these women in theory: in further parts, inserting them into her own texts. There she lays them and plays with them, to see what happens when she holds them in her sights. She moves around their various angles and orientations with her own. Just as well as one could dress up as a stripper, you could dress your writing up with a theorist.

93.

Acker opens the self by loosening the signifying system, extending this. A provoking web of texts and dreams and the interplays, overlays of biographemes—mutual, prodding in encountering, encouraging each other, move, to uncover more—give rise to that eventual, mythic, metaphor of the *labyrinth*: which Acker comes to see as a potential form of all bodies and their writing. In contradistinction to her early prison metaphor, and her figuring of the mother as "a wall," this bodily store is not such a bad place to be, get lost in, wonder: it non-threateningly holds, because one has a large part, hand in designing it. One concedes the goodness, full of twists and turns.

94.

As I fear I am getting a little too close for my own comfort to consolidating an argument around the *phallus*, which I don't want to do, let me go ahead and knock the wind out of my own sails in theory through poetry a bit, with a story. Gather round. I was in the galley, as it were, at the 2002 *Lust for Life* symposium, not presenting my own paper. Not accepted. Some people should not be put in bed together, as they say. I will not list all the participants here, but I refer the curious to Scholder's preface to the subsequently produced collection. I was among the audience, and I believe they visibly blanched, when thought lines of subversive "phallus" language use (à la Judith Butler's, the lesbian one, this time) were taken to serious extreme and end, quite gleefully though, by Chris Kocela: inserted again and again into Acker's *Pussy, King of the Pirates*, as one interpretive skeleton key. I thought it was funny, to not dismiss also basically bought it. I have ambivalences, when it comes to too much dry or high-minded theory. Perhaps distasteful. We went to lunch. I believe the group was Amy Scholder, the painter Judie Bamber, artist Nayland Blake, writer Ann Rower, and myself. I should add that it was only through Scholder's intervention I was even allowed to sit in the audience of the symposium, librarian intent on barring me from the premises for not registering prior. The librarian did like my getup, though, and said so: the skirt I thought was like one in a Wolfgang Tillmans photograph, the fluffy red sweater I still wore leftover from Michael Stipe days, silver shadow. But, yeah, over sake and noodles it's agreed, I mean, she was just hanging out with all these girls in dyke bars, back then when she was writing in San Francisco the book in question. Grant that this is in large part what Acker means by an insistence that writing always be brought back to the material body. It is also in effect the diary function, where poetry takes flight. Put the two together, through lots of hoops and stays—rhetorical language all tricked out, joins, jointed parts—and you have, in essence, what becomes the Acker novel.

95.

The scene of the strip-dance becomes one where she has no need to fabricate further perception. POLITICS: *we still had time left so I danced naked Ike and Tina Turner's RESPECT he yelled at me to get on the floor in the doggie position I did immediately got up he said do it you're supposed to do whatever I say I did it looked up at him and went rrrf-rrf rrrf-rrf the shits broke up I started crying again I want to go home to mommy you stupid cunt I want to see my mommy you're a brute I don't want to be married to you any longer.* In *Empire of the Senseless*, "In other words, the primal urge of sex had become a revolting phenomenon." Acker must make a new sense of what the experience has shown her. Acker sees a world of sexual commerce as still business of the capitalist, controlled by and for men, and she can no longer just accept this order as "normal," the further she sees. EMPIRE: *Here language was degraded.* As Daddy enters into "the demimonde of fake public sex, his speech turned from the usual neutral and acceptable journalese most normal humans use as a stylus mediocris into… His language went through an indoctrination of nothingness, for sexuality had no more value in his world, until his language no longer had sense." Paradoxically this strip-scene becomes Acker's site of authenticity, even if she is using the stories of other women she worked with, or surprisingly finds herself around. Consequently, she learns to wield it as an authorization for her view of world relations between commerce, sex and art. She puts a foot down on grounds of the time she feels she's done, sentence served, prompts questioning of positions through equivalencies she establishes. "Marcia" (or Janis Joplin) is reduced to street chanteuse to feed James Dean. In *Pussy, King of the Pirates*, "I looked glam, but the truth is, when I was in the sex biz, I wasn't. Sex biz is low and sleazy."

96.

Acker gussies herself up as sailor, pirate, engine harnesser on motorcycle-back, word wrangler and freer. Her books are collaborations fashioned between her memories, her daily existence she tries hard to make anything but unimaginative, her past books, her past stories she has told about herself, past words, words of others as she comes across them, and her own subsequent, changing through them. What Acker tries to bring forth in her books are new visions of herself and for herself. Through her dreaming-playing, masquerading or raging, her trying on of roles, her attempts to show the *nature* of society to be itself a blind appropriation, so unwittingly accepted— and secured further by the non-boat-rocking preservations of status quo gender conformity—Acker feeds herself and her fantasies in looping which becomes increasingly complex circuits over her career. I enter her pirate-sailor into analogy with Roland Barthes's "La Papillonne" fragment of working around work, getting around to work through a technique, technology of *cruising*. Traveling over the page, traveling over the body even while she writes, her appropriations pillage and critique society-culture-literature, yes, but they also, and most importantly, are aimed around pleasing her, moving back into the books forested around her, moving back out. Moving on to the keyboard, Acker drafts first in longhand then types the work up. Field reports. Picking up the pun Acker makes a conceit, highlighted in the title of *Hannibal Lecter, My Father*, we can see Acker's skinning of monuments, Daddy's, strutting her own exposure and production of language, politics in a highly theatrical flaunting exposing them for the flimsily disguised props they are, creating new uses for these old coverings, a poetics.

97.

I would like to give some further sense of what Bellamy's exhibition brought back to me, body now absent, pieces of Kathy Acker's wardrobe strung up, above at varying heights from rafters in a gallery's side rooms, limp like marionettes shelled, or, resting with draped wings bats, extra flaps and coverings needed gathered, as for curtains for the windows or doors, a whole motley patchwork, like when you were embarking upon the makeshift dark in a tent of childhood respite. It brings back to me, in a moment almost *madeleine*-like, that accusation always of hiding up under my mother's skirt. But more than that I feel myself even further engendered in how nice things were never had. It feels impossible not to reach for them, entering into that curated space, brushing up against the Betsey Johnson tops, Vivienne Westwood bottoms, or tanks, slips, jackets, Comme des Garçons pieces, a Champion Sports Wear vest, gloves, Gaultier, Japanese designer flourishes, John Richmond's "Woman" label where the *A* in the midst of the gender designation is made like the one the punks trademarked for anarchy, the letter's lean-to, barred support, surrounded with their circle. I walked up under the garments hanging, being dominated again by them, being a boy on the floor of my mother's wardrobe to hide, in trying to also be included. Some of the shifts in the breeze caused by my own body twisted and turned puppet-like strings. My sister played more acceptably with her in front of a dresser, jewelry and the makeup. It gets to be too irresistible with my feelings in there alone to not just grab at what I could reach with my own hands and something touch.

98.

The actor Acker, reader, experiences the making of new horizons as both a vocation and a medium, material. Others—immured as one may be in words—can become jarring space. Am *I* mother? Am *I* daughter? Who is "I," if not wanting to be other? Or must *I* be both and all to myself? It is one particular strand in Acker's work that could go under wording of *the psychoanalytic imagination*, a provocative, generative issue of textual practice in Acker's continued assembly of many. To make a new novel text, or poetry, upon foundational grounds of another, Acker grafts her own processing logic over prior enunciations, laying out the disconcerting aspects of her reading experiences, own identification of concerns, in more, further, words. Call this a written-out exploration of what happens to your narrative when you never saw or want to see your family as a triangle valid in and of itself to begin with, once the drama in many ways begins to move from a sublimated one, when the one who takes up the writing does not see the recovery of family primary concern. "The Birth of the Wild Heart," section 5: *Entering the true Heart—who am I now?*

99.

Among those poetic excursions I find in her Duke archive and place chronologically towards the end of her life are pieces that might have been joined to others, these loose sheaves of paper, through one of her past techniques or some new one, slipped by her into another book, that place to collect the working out done by her over a next period of compositional time, shored up further in some overarching conceit, another family of artists, made into more of a whole, or hole, through dream, vision, become one facet of a larger work, project, environment, or they might have been more simply forgotten. The focus now at the end of this life will be turned down to a couple of barer conceptual frames, in single pages of typed sheets. Here quite stark is the quandary of the lyric. Who calls out to whom? How will each of the two points constitute, separations to become a part of the other, through the other:

Mother and infant
Infant and mother
I/you want I/you

Try to establish who comes first, in "I/you."

100.

She will do it too with the symbolism play sung between Orpheus or "OR" or Eurydice called: *YOU.* Try to establish priorities, which one of needs to be more taken—priorities: how one looks through the other, to see oneself cared for or not. Who provides the grounds for treading upon for whose story? For sustenance, guidance, nourishment metaphorical or otherwise, which is in more need of the other—determining of who follows whom, which taken hand.

Mother and infant
Infant and mother
Which way to the full land?

Mother and infant
Infant and mother
Safe in the imaginary space

101.

In those notebooks published as "The Birth of the Wild Heart": *I am a child of the forests and the wilds; I am all that is American.* Kraus pulls from a notebook in which Acker is drafting the piece on copyright to appear in MMLA: *Loneliness—it's the American way.* Particular attention is given to this *American* in Acker's last notebooks: "American, as they say. What does that mean? I kick butt with the best of them. I can't hold myself in. Not sex, not anyway. The wild heart." Acker goes over her story of origins again, a primal scene. *Four months later when she tried to*—"abort" is typed as "about me"—*I learned that I was hated and to hate myself, we were the same; most of all I hated myself for not busting out of that womb, not shoving my foot into the mucus membrane and there tearing a hole and emerging, emerging into light and woods, me American, because before her and him.*

233

102.

The psychoanalysts ("Kathy hated psychoanalysis," Matias said, 3/18/15, as we were looking together through some of her starting notebooks, newly acquired by Fales Library): they have much to say about the daughter's difficulty in separating herself out from her mother, and so does Acker, just as much late in her life as very early on. She writes in viewing a scene of desire, commenting on what she is in the process of creating, in *The Childlike Life of the Black Tarantula by the Black Tarantula*, "I can't decide whether I'm a woman giving birth to a brat or a five-year-old girl." She is channeling her creation here through the Violette Leduc work, *Thérèse and Isabelle*, a favorite, theorizing the possibilities of subtext in a lesbian romance. Which one is the girl I am? Who is *mommy* now? In *I Dreamt I Was a Nymphomaniac*, she writes, "Monster women surrounded me all the time. Now I hate women and sentimentality." Whose book holds whom, what? PORTRAIT: *I read Sartre De Sade Laing Esterson and Leduc. I'm scared I don't have my own space.*

103.

Keep having new people (identities) being born. Surrounded by delusions, vary your (material) conditions along the way: "poor," "crazy," "man," "woman." PORTRAIT: *my family thinks of itself as aristocratic, though it isn't, since my grandmother (mother's mother) came from Alsace-Lorraine to U.S.A. poor and in her later life married a wealthy man.* Trapped in a life, keep having the dreams. PORTRAIT: *My mother wanted to make me exactly like her.* Pick someone new to be, a new time and place to begin, to start out differently from, spring. (Imprisoned, more literally, "1789 [ ] On account of my pro-Revolutionary attitude, they move me from my prison at Vincennes…. I'm concerned with my personal freedom I'm not insane by my standards.") This was one of the strategies to keep a narrative, penniless, motherless, beginning, going. PORTRAIT: *I move to New York because I write and I want to meet writers. I have no money…no parents.* My ellipses. She writes, before going on to try to channel Sade, "I'm trying to become other people because this is what I find interesting." At a loss for direction, "Only interest in the ideas of the Marquis." Before the line breaks, no period, and the following paragraph commences, instructs herself, commands, towards the end in another section, *The Childlike Life of the Black Tarantula*: "Redo myself."

104.

The metaphors of semiotics become freighted for Acker, as she's first literalized as a site of restrictions. The mother, in her *Great Expectations*, "had always been very tight with me: taking away my allowances, never buying me anything." In a folder for the typescript of 1981's "The Birth of the Poet," a page from one of Acker's notebooks, trimmed around a text headed THE INVISIBLE: *There is something called the countryside tho I never see it. / I know the flowers of shade and the flowers of water. Bloodstones and St. John's Cross, waterlilies every kind of red rose. I have learned that there are birds of the evening and of the night, bats, owls, screechers, babies fallen out of their nests and drowned in a bucket. They haunt my dreams. A willow again closes its branches around me,*—and this passage there cuts off.

105.

An admission from Carolee Schneemann, that Acker's mother "was a bad breast." This was during the *Lust for Life* symposium. Not having known Acker personally, I will not be on certain points quite so assured as others. Also at this time was the confirmation or announcement friend Bob Glück made during his slot. He told us who she was in one of her books, the character under whose name she moved, and also where courtesy of her he was making his appearance, based on what he had told her in a conversation they had once had. In her version of *Great Expectations*, Acker is "Cynthia," I think he said. In *Kathy Goes to Haiti*, 1978: "The boy writes his name and address on the first page of *Desolation Angels*." I am one who sees her characters in line with those semi-autobiographical portraits the Beats could be so fond of, Kerouac as Jack Duluoz in the "Legend of Duluoz" books, Leo Percepied in *The Subterraneans*, Ray Smith in *The Dharma Bums*, Peter Martin in *The Town and the City*, Sal Paradise in *On the Road*, and Mike Ryko in the once unpublished manuscript "And the Hippos Were Boiled in Their Tanks," co-authored with William Burroughs writing as William Lee. Kathy says, "I like Kerouac but he worked too much from intuition for me.... Burroughs really was doing the major work because he was dealing with how politics and language come together..." Acker worked on how language and identity, and then by extension the politics of self-selecting communities, came together.

106.

In the *Burning Bombing* suite, "WE HAVE NOTHING AMERICA [ ] DOESN'T THAT HAVE TO DO WITH

EVERYTHING? WE HAVE NO GRAIN [ ] I FIND GRAIN [ ]
I PROPOSITION THE GRAIN [ ] GRAIN COMING [ ] OUT
OF THE MOTHER." Her mother's child, casting herself out,
Acker will work to reflect identification through conceptions of
how one becomes aligned, how one is marked, importing large
areas of her understanding from outside, for example from un-
American Genet. In his memoir, *Prisoner of Love*, he finds, "In
white America the Blacks are the characters in which history is
written. They are the ink that gives the white page a meaning."
The human imagination tries to get away. Do we hold onto the
words or do we let them go? She does not ever exactly come out
anywhere to say she is of the school that racial difference is a
fiction, and indeed it may be one of her privileges that she never
had to provide such. In *Pussy, King*, magic is named "black" by
the local politicians. Enlightenment is for control. In *Blood and
Guts in High School*: "You, the thing called 'you,' was a ball
turning and turning in the blackness only the blackness wasn't
something—like 'black'—and it wasn't nothingness 'cause
nothingness was something." Before her consolidation of the
character of the abandoned, abused, controlled subject, a note
toward composition among the drafts in notebooks marked for
her "Jeanne Duval" prompts to remember of what will be valued
in creation for her: *Who am I? black*. Duval may be grounded in
history, but what is in a name? A color? She sets her "Algeria,"
which will *invoke*, call out, *because nothing else works*, on the
eve of the Algerian Revolution, much like Genet's *The Screens*,
before he moves on to his alliance with the Black Panthers,
before his work with Palestine. This is different than some
romance around "becoming Kerouac." If language is said to
correspond with reality if she used it differently could she have
a hand in changing that? What of Omar being female? (What of

Leroi Jones becoming Baraka, distancing himself, calling out Baldwin as, "Joan of Arc of the cocktail party"?) Sex for her is good because it breaks out of a prison of the rational mind. This is especially true for the disinherited. Life in America "stinks." Algeria is pink. The "black" becomes one with the dark which is in her logic of inversion a good place to be. Stored away in a *Childlike* notebook, in the Fales Library collection of her early bits: *Blackness. I am blackness. I'm alive.* (PUSSY, KING: *In solitude so complete that it approached nothingness, she'd meditate on whiteness. Which is nothingness.*) Notice this is not the complete eschewing of any identity, but the trying on of another. I concede though some words can be taken off at will and provisional. ("Persian Poems," inserted into the mix of *Blood and Guts*: "a woman is a dirty/ black head.) Tattoos are harder to remove. Appropriation? Self-loathing? It is also hard but important to sustain a reading of the words, like *black*, let us say, in Acker's corpus, as the usage and points from which these issue shift between the covers. This is not a sullying, but a starting out point. Naïve, perhaps. Like a child. Reductive or an alliance, traditions are being contested. Appearance becomes a marker. She does not want to pass as white. She does not want to pretend that white is neutral. The men in a bar in *Nymphomaniac* come up to the "I"; they tell her she's O.K., an evaluation accompanied by an epithet, how her haircut ("I had short curly hair all over my head") made her look like their slur.

107.

In her analysis, Kristeva situates a realm of abjections and how an ego is or isn't formed in the face of a big "O," other the mother does or does not become. In her book *Melanie Klein*, volume two of her "Female Genius" trilogy, Kristeva explains: "*ab-ject*, with this *a* understood in the privative sense of the prefix, that is, as vitiating the object as well as the emerging subject. It is a subject and object that, as such, are crystallized only through what Klein calls the 'depressive position' or, strictly speaking, through the castration ordeal, the resolution of the Oedipus conflict, and the creative acquisition of language and thought." She then goes on to assert something I am more concerned with than through Klein the reincorporation of gendered dynamics of Oedipus and family triangles. A link to the potential function of modern art ("difficulties posed," Kristeva puts it) is made, as analogous to states of the sacred and mystic in their bearings upon limit states of sublimation, what we do or do not allow ourselves to see or know or feel or try to control, conceive, or this at least is how I interpret the given assertion. Kristeva herself refers us back to pages in earlier books of hers. We experience the states again like the narcissistic one of early object relation. The mother/infant unit has not yet been fully divided in the infant's mind into the family by the entrance of Symbolization. Names like the Father, etc. The realm before the triangles begin is made up of terms that become defined through genders. It is presumed a child's "successful," clear-cut emergence from this is through identifying with one or the other of the two. Kristeva drives this point home: *Like a band in a Möbius strip that is characterized by its limitlessness, the future subject is forever transported toward the "ab-ject" (on the side of the mother) and toward "primary identification" with the "father of personal prehistory" (on the side of the loved and loving and pre-oedipal father, who displays the traits of both parents)....* Here is how in Acker difficultly lodges before the poles are established, before they bring with them all they engender. In her writing, even the womb is a dangerous and unloving place to begin the subject, already mediating the (unseen) father. In "The Birth of the Wild Heart," section four: *I know what it's like now to be in that womb all squashed especially my left arm, and she finds out, the woman who is me, the woman who is outside me, she learns that he is going to leave her.* Father cut out, mother pains. Avital Ronell's contribution to the *Lust for Life* book, "Kathy Goes to Hell: On the Irresolvable Stupidity of Acker's Death," brings in Klein, too. In "The Good Breast" section of it, Ronell recognizes Acker analogously: "And like all good breasts, she invites ambivalence and poisoning, a reflex of destruction, as you saw occurring in the first lines of my homage to her." Klein "vexed" Freud, to quote Ronell more, when she "backdated aggression, making one ready to rocket after just a few weeks of this existence."

108.

Acker creates in her work a place where it is difficult to separate the theory from what the writing becomes. Her list of "Ten Out of Many Women Writers," "a list of writers who are female whose work matters to me," a list which she clarifies is in no order of importance—*I don't think like that*— includes a number eleven, added for Emily Brontë. In copying the list from the Duke Archive, I had noted for her number eleven "Emily Dickinson." This must have been in my haste to get down as much as possible of all that excited me in the couple of days I had in Durham, North Carolina, to work through Acker's papers. Passing by another copy of the list at a later date, in the Serpent's Tail/High Risk Archive in Fales at NYU, I amend my original notation. Fales has been invaluable to my development as writer. Perhaps the manuscript exists in two versions.

109.

Like anyone else, that Virgin must get her makeover in Acker. PORTRAIT: *I hallucinate that the Virgin Mary wears black leather pants and a black leather motorcycle jacket, she climbs trees, she doesn't give a fuck for anyone.* Her functioning in society changes. Elsewhere, she is an image to which people give trinkets that symbolize their problems and that they've bought right outside the church in Merida, the main city in the Yucatan, where protagonist ten-year-old Janey Smith lives with her father. BLOOD AND GUTS: *an arm is a broken arm, a baby is problems with baby, a kidney, a little worker.* Or she is sought out to resolve, absolve problems. IDENTITY: *In order to repent my matricide, I walked into Notre Dame, it was nighttime, and pissed on the statue of the Virgin Mary.* She gives rise to circuitous logic and instincts. DON: *Religious white men hate women because and so they make women into the image of the Virgin Mary.* SENSELESS: *A guy was hugging a wood statue of the Virgin then he pierced the Statue's cunt, if the Virgin had a cunt, with his knife he threw himself on Her his teeth biting Her cheeks and bruised lips, he asked Her to fuck him.* Or she becomes just another sign, public. In HAITI: *Virgin Mary's La Sirene's Jesus Christ's Duvalier's private girlfriends' names adorn every inch of the bus' walls.* She becomes an issue of distinction, one that will lead to violence. SENSELESS, again: *I would have Mary Magdalene tear Virgin Mary's flesh into shreds.* An alienating principle, *In Memoriam to Identity*, she is: *'Since I'm not the Virgin Mary, God, You hate me.'*

IDENTITY: *The mother came to realize that she wasn't the Virgin Mary though she was a mother.* IDENTITY: *He was unable to relate to anyone except for the Virgin Mary and Jesus Christ.* IDENTITY: *For his wife was the Virgin Mary who must never, under any circumstances, be bothered, disturbed, or agitated, especially by such a foul thing as sex, in especial by R's homosexuality.* IDENTITY: *'Every night do you bend down and worship your wife, the Virgin Mary?'* MOTHER: *One result of this journey, or 'identity,' could be my loss of interest in 'feminine power.' Images of the Eternal Mother, the Virgin Mary, etc.* DON: *I, all females who're isolated, am the Virgin.* MOTHER: *I look like Madonna fucking. (She took me through two more dye jobs.)*

110.

The tenth woman on Acker's list of many women writers is in her words: "The Mother of Us All: Gertrude Stein." *Her meditative stance in writing—her insistence on breath, her refusal to subordinate any part of the narrative text to any other part, her refusal to exist in writing anywhere but in a calm which is joy—is an implicit rejection of the later 19th century myth that the artist must suffer in order to create. Writers and others have yet to explore and use her work.* Laying aside those Acker seems so ready to do like the $L=A=N=G=U=A=G=E$ poets in considering those who have or have not explored and used in her mind Stein's work, we can trace this joy. She is in *The Burning Bombing of America* in a line: *I lonely praise you [ ] Gertrude Stein [ ] Walt Whitman [ ] Allen Ginsberg [ ] the women of you.* It is a joy that Acker is trying to move to accentuate repeatedly throughout the 90s, in a decade corresponding with her desire to begin making, for herself, new myths within which to try to live. I want to try to end more on a note of it, emphasizing it here in a quote from her "Allen Ginsberg—A Personal Portrait," another piece in her Papers. "In these times which seem to be increasingly dominated by nightmares which are the interiorizations of the media-government alliance, there must be an opening into joy. Whatever that means and however that must be accomplished." It could even be like quoting in its entirety in the midst of an essay she is to write William Blake's poem "Infant Joy," to create the *Low* piece she did. She is not alone. "The Birth of the Wild Heart," section 1: *Dante called for help and then he went thro pain and reached joy.* "The Birth of the Wild Heart," section 2: *Why do you deprive the body? The body wants sex, that is its joy, not namby-pamby little holier-than-thou—but joy full and in the face.*

111.

In the imaginary space that might let all spring up—but is still just that, at this point, "imaginary"—the haunting refrain, rocking, of only two points, two legs to designs not yet fully emerged formed. Kristeva would call this sacred space, the space of a mother still holding, containing, the child. In one of her illustrations, the leap of her Mary and her Christ child iconic, staged. "Part Two" of Acker's 1997 work "Requiem" is called "Christmas." We witness the hold Acker's mother obviously still possesses on her child, as she returns to her again. This time she is at the center of the drama. The daughter at a point finds Agatha Christie and pornography in a hall closet. The character Claire says to her daughter: *We're all we've got, Electra. We've got to stick together.* A month later, in the play, Claire is dead and "Electra" sees her first dead body on Christmas Day. From that same year, in "Eurydice in the Underworld": *It is Christmas Day when all the world goes under the earth.* "E" replies to Orpheus's letter, relating, accusing: *You said, 'I'm not in this world in order to take care of you.'*

112.

To quote, and to begin to bastardize a bit too, that thinker you see I do love to play around with, Barthes, his "*Langue / Tongue*" fragment from *The Pleasure of the Text*: "No object is in a constant relationship with pleasure (Lacan, apropos of Sade)." Entering further through Barthes's parenthetical clarification, I find Lacan's name a couple times in Acker's work. In addition to "Russian Constructivism" he is in, and the quote in *My Mother*, Lacan is cited in the back of a working notebook for *Pussy, King of the Pirates*: "the mirror-image is 'the threshold of the visible world'." Identity or the book and how they mutually construct each other in the worlds of Acker will be one such object that provides transition to, through, pleasures. If not Lacan, Acker placed great, evidential store we know in Sade. Dennis Cooper, co-editor of the Acker reader with Scholder, is instructive in an interview with Robert Glück: "Sade's work identifies its enemies and uses the construction of these enemies' principles and rhetoric in the construction of its own narratives and philosophy." Cooper goes on, "My work doesn't see itself as having enemies. I would never put myself in a class with Sade, as a writer or as a thinker, God knows." Rather than exclaim over that God, I will say rather Acker I believe would. She deserves this. I should perhaps point out more explicitly some of the things Acker locates herself in Sade, when writing on him. To not give the appearance of having wandered too far afield. Letting Barthes lead me through Acker to Cooper, I am willing to entertain I may display, attempt to hide, or act out, compensate for my *castration anxiety* refusing to stick to one body or point of consolidated meaning. Freedom is equated with despising the mother and virginity. "The daughter who does not reject her mother interiorizes prison," Kathy Acker writes in her essay on Sade. What does the critic do who is leery of trying to get too tight a handle on her? Acker begins making a mythic use of theory, as she relies on her evolving "theory" too of myth, interrogating and refashioning who holds strings or the threads leading into and out of our stories of our selves. "Reading the Lack of the Body: The Writing of the Marquis de Sade": *A woman invariably gives up any hope of freedom, mentions the older woman, as soon as she has a child. A woman who wants to be free, above all, must avoid pregnancy.* Both sodomy and abortion figure heavily in this program.

113.

Barthes goes on in his fragment of a sustained relation to pleasure, "For the writer, however, this object does exist: it is not the language, it is the *mother tongue*. The writer is someone who plays with ["his"—her/the/a] mother's body...." Emphasis in the original. Barthes follows his assertion to in parentheses bring in the source of his phrasing, citing further now the names of two writers, one of which is Lautréamont, and then the painter Matisse. Larry McCaffery gives a lineage, an alternative one to be sure, in an interview, "Well,

Lautréamont's influence created almost a straight line to Dada, Surrealism, Burroughs, punk, and Kathy Acker." It is the abject we might make our meanings in the face of, that we define, that on a gut level we want to keep outside of or are taught to and see from ourselves as distinct. The words on a page darken in. They have their backings, which can also be distorted. "The Birth of the Wild Heart," section 2: "Remember that time, one of your most precious memories, where the trees bowed to you and said, 'You are now the princess.'" When is the dark forest preferable to a white field? When you are not in it alone. LOW: *Through the walls, the children could hear their parents planning their deaths.* They link together. The "beautiful forest" is brought in from other countries or books. Opening another diary, "The Birth of the Wild Heart," section 5: *Making the world into a womb.* She wanted to set out upon the white page to get away from signs of "fixed," already determined significance, though she needed also those signs she wanted to leave behind to steer her course, away.

114.

"Every time I ran away from school and walked into the Village, home of the Beats, I felt an edge of fear that isn't fear but the beginning of passion and of joy and I knew, even though I didn't really know these people yet, that I wanted to spend the rest of my life in this new world of openness." She writes in this manuscript of "Allen Ginsberg—A Personal Portrait": *All of us come from parents. My parents were not my biological parents; they were the poets.* And, her emphasis: *poetry's only rule is that it is not about, it is joy.* Ibid: *No voice. / But, I'm going to write. / And I did and I am writing. And doing everything around writing.* She classifies herself as a woman who "does not want to be a male, or a judge, to tell people how to think, who only wants to disappear, to go under, to subvert." She says how her writing "became, if you like something else." PERSONAL PORTRAIT: "Became, formally at least, a writing that is dispersed and that disperses, disperses narrative, gender, genre, character, language is always moving away from itself anyway…until, and this is what I want, subversion turns over subversion into joy." And I struggle with the last sentence, being the last note, wanting to let it both resound more and to leave it in her hands as she runs away.

Afterword Note

Papers in the text marks the Duke Location. NYU resources, denoted variously, include the Serpent's Tail/High Risk Archive and Downtown Collection at the Fales Library. If it is not immediately clear, italicized portions in the text are quoted materials. Excerpts from published and unpublished writings courtesy of the Kathy Acker Literary Trust. I want to thank Stephen for publishing this with Nightboat Books, enlarging audience, and all there along with him who have helped with this manuscript.

Acker's self-styling is historically situated. Often I wonder what she would be doing or saying if she were here in this moment. I do not imagine she would have gotten any sweeter. She did not live to see Obama's America, Facebook, social hashtag uprisings, the fear of civil liberties attacks impending yet again, Presidential tweets, hate fore-fronted in the dealings of business bullying terms. People ask me if I ever met her. I provide more or less information depending on the particular setting. The chance to talk to her as she was dying was extended to me.

I did not take the opportunity to call the hospital. I had begun reading her books in the late nineties to try to move out of a heartbreak, as I felt a sense of self aligned with a development of hers. This was before I knew personally Amy Scholder, Lynne Tillman, Robert Glück, Kevin Killian; before I had approached Dodie Bellamy in appreciation, before I listened to what Eileen Myles told me about my subject on a book tour they shared.

This work has a long history, and like any book that comes to be, there are many possible starting points. The mentoring affection and belief Colm Tóibín held in me for my first book is still immeasurable. As far back as 2005, while Sarah Schulman and I were both advisors at Goddard College, she heavily encouraged me to continue bringing Acker's work into what I was doing, to teach Acker, and to ask others to consider Kathy. It was at Sarah's suggestion that I was first in touch with Matias Viegener. There were not yet any full-length studies of Acker's life or books on the horizon when I began the writing. Many thanks to him for everything over all these many years now. Talks with Kate Zambreno over the last couple of years have also been sustaining, imbued with a sense of eye-to-eye. At the MoMA *Cine Virus* evening reception, Cecilia Doughtery and I conversed in great detail over her own Acker writing. Sylvère Lotringer interacted warmly with me when Brandon Stosuy made introductions at the *Up Is Up But So Is Down* launch, and that is something to cherish.

It has been galvanizing and in some exchanges edifying to be in occasional correspondence with Chris Kraus, beginning the summer of 2013 with wondering first how she could get a copy of my dissertation (*When She Does What She Does: Intertextual Desire and Influence in Kathy Acker's Narratives*), defended 2007 to a committee of Wayne Koestenbaum, Eve Kosofosky Sedgwick, and Ammiel Alcalay. She had been planning to write about her critics. A couple of years later again for leads to facts with a few questions, read it again, finding it newly informative and valuable. I took also her criticism to heart (*some of the hagiographic stuff really difficult, as if no woman had ever written an avant garde book before her - which does a disservice to where KA went with her sources and influences*). To paraphrase a bit from a talk she gave at the New School: *Every girl then and every girl now feels it speaks to her*. Me too. As I began to try to move study from conception and realization at the CUNY Graduate Center, Juliana Spahr gave a generous early read and offered insights into its staging and lines that it was straddling. Robert Reid-Pharr and I had greeted each other often in the school's hallways, and though I took no classes with him (his seminar on Delany could have been vital here), one provocation he expressed moderating a panel I attended indelibly affected my thinking. What if some words just went away?

Interactions with Wayne have continued to be nourishing and a point to the type of thinking and writing and creation one might do within the institutions I still find myself needing to make my way. It has been devastating to lose the presence of Eve, who made a space for so much. The key was the enjoyment was to be primary. At Wesleyan University, since 2008 with various contractual appointments I have held versions of, tenuously and with near constant trepidation, my work's situation between the experimental and critical and pedagogy has to date been most vocally supported through Matthew Garrett. His friendship continues to shape and inspire, along with a constellation of others there. Ruth Nisse has given much vigilant and enriching care and intellectual stimulation; Lily Saint a reassurance plus history.

It was while still in Georgia (Athens) that I saw my first Acker book, in a place called Stovepipe, a storefront to the side of a coffee house I worked and wrote at when there were the lulls. My reaction was dismissive, the cutting edge so obviously marketed, the design of being ripped. Until it was for Toby, then the only thing he had with him in his bag he could offer me to read.

Quoted Publications by Kathy Acker

Don Quixote, which was a Dream, Grove Press, 1986

Blood and Guts in High School, Grove Press, 1989

Empire of the Senseless, Grove Press, 1989

Great Expectations, Grove Press, 1989

Literal Madness (Kathy Goes to Haiti; My Death My Life by Pier Paolo Pasolini; Florida), Grove Press, 1989

In Memoriam to Identity, Grove Press, 1990

Hannibal Lecter, My Father, Semiotext(e), 1991

Portrait of An Eye (The Childlike Life of the Black Tarantula by the Black Tarantula; I Dreamt I Was a Nymphomaniac; The Adult Life of Toulouse-Lautrec by Henri Toulouse-Lautrec), Grove Press, 1992

My Mother: Demonology, Grove Press, 1994

Pussy, King of the Pirates, Grove Press, 1996

Bodies of Work: Essays, Serpent's Tail, 1997

Eurydice in the Underworld, Arcadia Books, 1997

Rip-off Red, Girl Detective and the Burning Bombing of America: The Destruction of the U.S., Grove Press, 2002

Formatting Notes

[ ] denotes irregular spacing in original manuscript
/ designates paragraph breaks within quoted passages

I have kept misspellings and possible sic's in published books, while amending some in quoted correspondence and unpublished manuscripts.

About the Author

Douglas A. Martin is the author of eight books across genres, including volumes of poetry and fiction. His most recent novel is *Once You Go Back*. Other titles include *Your Body Figured* and *They Change the Subject*. He divides his time between Greenpoint, Brooklyn and a kit home in Callicoon, New York where he lives with the artist Bobby Abate, their dog and a Tuxedo Russian Blue.

Nightboat Books

Nightboat Books, a nonprofit organization, seeks to develop audiences for writers whose work resists convention and transcends boundaries. We publish books rich with poignancy, intelligence, and risk. Please visit our website, nightboat.org, to learn about our titles and how you can support our future publications.

The following individuals have supported the publication of this book. We thank them for their generosity and commitment to the mission of Nightboat Books:

Elizabeth Motika
Benjamin Taylor

In addition, this book has been made possible, in part, by grants from The National Endowment for the Arts and The New York State Council on the Arts Literature Program.